CROQUET

(ASSOCIATION CROQUET)

A Handbook on the Strokes and Tactics of the Game.

Also a Short Description of Golf and Polo or Robber Croquet

BY

The Rev. G. F. HANDEL ELVEY, M.A.

PREFACE

In 1910 I wrote a short Handbook dealing exclusively with Croquet Strokes. Just after the first world war my little Book was revised and re-published, with chapters added on Break-making, Break-laying and the picking up of Breaks. In order to make the present volume more complete and of greater value, especially to beginners and medium players, Chapters are now included on the Tactics of the Game. I would, however, call the attention of readers to the fact that this is, and is intended to be, a small Handbook, not an exhaustive Treatise dealing with a very large number of possible situations. The general system of the Chapters on Break-making and the Tactics of the Game as a whole, is to explain to the reader carefully the principles on which successful croquet is based, with just a few examples, leaving him to exercise his own imagination in applying those principles to the many and various situations arising in actual play. Whatever hobby I have taken up I have obtained and read such instruction books as were available on the subject, and I have certainly gained much pleasure from such reading, as well as assistance for the task in hand; I therefore venture to hope that those who read this little book will also gain pleasure and profit.

G. F. HANDEL ELVEY.

CONTENTS

I	Introductory Remarks	6
II	Golf and Polo or Robber Croquet	11
III	Mallets	13
IV	Style	17
V	Hitting One's Own Ball	23
VI	Single Strokes	25
VII	Double Strokes	34
VIII	Break-making. Introductory	41
IX	The Four Ball Break	43
X	The Three Ball Break	48
XI	How to Pick up Breaks	56
XII	How to Lay Breaks	59
XIII	The Openings	63
XIV	Tactics of the Out-player	66
XV	The End of the Game	68
XVI	The Triple and Double Peels	70
XVII	Miscellaneous Tactical Advice	72
XVIII	The Taking of Bisques	74
XIX	Doubles	77
XX	Practice	79

INTRODUCTORY REMARKS

(*A few notes for the non-player, especially the non-player who might become a recruit if sufficiently interested.*)

CROQUET might aptly be described as a combative race-game. A race-game because the object of play is to "race" to the Peg, get there first, and peg-out; combative, because it is not merely a case of doing something better than the opponent, as in Golf, but of actively and persistently fighting him.

Historically, Croquet is quite probably, in fact, what some players have desired to call it, namely, "Lawn-Billiards." Since on good authority Billiards was once an outdoor game, and the earliest tables retained Croquet characteristics in the shape of a Peg—called "The King"—and a hoop on the centre line of the table. Be this as it may, Croquet has Billiards characteristics in that it depends on the making of breaks, and on angles. It has also a slight Chess element in the fact that a player has often to weigh up the possibilities as to the effect of a proposed course of action on the progress of the game. The argument often goes like this: "If I do so and so, and succeed, what shall I gain? But, if I fail, how much shall I give away to my opponent." But, of course, the special characteristic of Croquet that distinguishes it from all other games is the "Croquet-stroke" itself; the placing of the player's ball in contact with another and striking it so that both balls are moved. And the high art of the game, which contains a great deal of its fascination, is by practice to obtain such control that the Striker can send both balls to pre-determined positions.

A glance at the diagram will show that there are six hoops and a peg in the centre of the Court. The diagram also gives the order in which the hoops are taken, and their names. It will be noticed that there is the outward journey from Hoop 1 to Hoop 6, and the return journey from Hoop 1 back to the Rover Hoop. Further study of the diagram will show that there are two Baulk Lines, called respectively Baulk Line A and Baulk Line B.

The full-sized Court is 35 yards long and 28 yards wide.

A Diagram of the Court will be found on Page 30.

For purposes of private play the size of the Court may be proportionately reduced, except in one respect, namely, the distance from the Fourth and Second Corner Spots to the end of each Baulk Line respectively should be maintained at 13 yards. Thus if the size of the Court were reduced to 28 yards by 20 yards, the length of each Baulk Line would be 9 yards.

The beginner would be well advised to remember that just as the expert amateur Billiard player might play a game of 500 to 1,000 up, and the very ordinary player be satisfied with 100 up or even 50 up, so he should also be satisfied with a shorter game than the expert. To start with, he should certainly not attempt to do more than the outward journey, making Hoop 6 his " Rover Hoop " and going thence to the Peg. There is no doubt that the attempt of the raw beginner to play the full length game is detrimental both to the beginner and to the popularity of Croquet. It is foolish to attempt to run before you can walk. The full-length game is, in fact, far too long until some progress has been made in the art of picking up and making breaks. For the raw beginner to try to play the full-length game is like a fifty-up man at Billiards setting out to play a game of 1,000.

As in other pursuits, the best way of getting to know about it is to be shown by a friend who is a knowledgable enthusiast. Probably the worst way would be to try to learn from the Laws of Croquet. These Laws must of necessity be complicated, because they have to deal with the manifold and various situations that arise in tournament play, not only in this country but in Australia, New Zealand and South Africa. In the two former there are many thousands of players. Our English Croquet Association is the law-making body for the whole Croquet world, except America. The beginner therefore would be well advised, having read carefully Laws 1-8, giving the order of play, the dimensions of the Courts and the implements used, to treat the rest of the Laws as a book of Reference, to be kept in the pocket and be consulted as and when required.

As soon as the beginner has mastered the rudiments of the game he or she will find that a wonderful new and most fascinating pleasure has come into his life. It is a pleasure, too, that is open to old and young, and both sexes. Though, as in other games of skill, the fresh eyes of youth and supple muscles are a great advantage, so long as there is health and strength, age in itself is no bar against winning even high honour at Croquet. Surely it is no disadvantage to feel that when you are taking up a new hobby you are taking up a hobby that may be a delight to you for the rest of your life.

Admittedly, Croquet is not an athletic game; but neither for that matter are Bowls or Billiards, and yet there are many young Bowlers, and no one would think of suggesting that Billiards was not a game for young people.

Croquet, by the by, has numbered among its devotees men who have been international footballers, cricketers of high repute, splendid golfers and excellent lawn-tennis players. Therefore, when a young man or girl decides to make Croquet his or her second game, ready to hand for the time when athletic games become too strenuous, such can be well assured that they are following in the footsteps of great sportsmen and sportswomen.

In this chapter we have been trying to kindle the enthusiasm of possible recruits, and to warn such as to certain pitfalls that might damage it. If we have succeeded in interesting him or her—and we hope this will prove to be the case—the following chapters will be found to show clearly how to play the standard strokes of the game, how to make Breaks, pick up Breaks and lay Breaks, and will give a general knowledge of the Tactics of the Game—both the Tactics of the In-player and the Tactics of the Out-player.

We hope that all readers of this little book will find things to interest them; and we specially hope that, as they read, possible recruits will be enthused to become keen beginners.

The following short synopsis has been published by the Croquet Association:—

Croquet—a Simple Synopsis.

Croquet is played with four balls, Blue and Black *v.* Red and Yellow. In starting the game each ball plays in turn from one of the two inner lines termed baulks. Thereafter the sides, but not necessarily the colours of that side, play alternately.

Both balls of a side must score all points to win. A ball propelled through its hoop by the action of another ball may score the point.

The four outside hoops (No. 1 having a blue cross-bar) are first scored, then 5 and 6 in the centre. They are subsequently scored the reverse way from the 2nd, which becomes 1 back, to the 6th (now called the penultimate), then the Rover (with red cross-bar), and finally the winning peg is hit. The coloured clips indicate the objective hoop, and are placed on the crown for 1 to 6 and on the upright for 1 back to rover.

A turn a stroke or series of strokes, extra ones being earned by:—

(1) Hitting another ball with your own ball (making a "roquet"). The two balls are then placed in contact, the player takes croquet from the other ball and is then entitled to make a further stroke.

(2) Passing through (running) a hoop.

The player may take croquet from each ball once during his turn, but may not do so a second time in the same turn unless meantime he has run a hoop. By a combination of taking croquet and running hoops, several or all the hoops can be scored by the player in one turn. This is called "making a break." In a four ball break three other balls are used. In a three ball break two of them. In a two ball break, one.

It will be apparent that the player wishes to use or control as many balls as possible himself, and to prevent the opponent from doing so. For these reasons most players start by going to a corner, or side boundary, as the fourth ball to start is the only one that really has a chance of an immediate break. The second player often plays his ball about 7 yards out from A baulk, hoping the third will shoot at it (and miss!) instead of joining the partner. The third player frequently takes this shot, as, should he hit, he can lay the balls in such manner as to give him the chance of a break, should the fourth ball fail to hit. During a game, if a break is not feasible, players sometimes elect to go to a corner or boundary to make the opponent's turn more difficult.

A turn is concluded when the player has made all the strokes to which he is entitled, or if he fail to make a roquet, or run a hoop, or if when taking croquet he sends either ball over the boundary. The turn also ceases if the player makes an illegal stroke or "foul" as defined in the Laws.

In handicap games, the weaker player receives a defined number of extra turns or bisques, which may be taken singly or in succession at the end of a turn. A half bisque is an extra turn in which no point may be scored.

II

GOLF AND POLO OR ROBBER CROQUET

JUST as given a Billiards Table, other games are available as well as official Billiards; so given a Croquet Court, other games can be played on it as well as Association Croquet, and this is in fact the case. Two of these may be briefly touched on here. Golf Croquet and Polo or Robber Croquet.

In Golf Croquet there are no extra turns, and no taking of Croquet. As in Golf, the players play for each hole in turn, so in Golf Croquet the players play for each Hoop until it is made, and until a Hoop has been run, no player is allowed to send his ball to the next Hoop. The balls are played in sequence—Blue, Red, Black, Yellow. The start is made from Baulk B. The Peg does not come into Golf Croquet, instead, after the Rover Hoop, the Third Hoop—called in Golf Croquet Hoop 13—is contested as the Final Point. Golf Croquet can be played in Singles or Partnership, in each case Blue and Black versus Red and Yellow. What is written in the following pages about Hoop-running, aiming, playing to a given spot, is all applicable to Golf Croquet as well as Association Croquet. The Laws of Golf Croquet are published by the Croquet Association with the Laws of Association Croquet.

The advantages of Golf Croquet are that it is very easy to learn. The games are quick and there are no long turns.

Polo or Robber Croquet is an excellent game for the odd half-hour. The following is a very brief description of it:—

The balls are played from Baulk Line A, and each ball must run the First Hoop before it becomes a Free Ball. As soon as it has become a Free Ball it can score Points and make Roquets—that is, it can hit other balls. When a player hits the Peg, or runs a Hoop, or makes Roquet, he is entitled to another stroke. When a Free Ball or an Alive Ball runs a Hoop, two is added to the score; if it hits the Peg, one is added to the score. A player having run a Hoop or hit the Peg cannot run the same Hoop (the reverse way) or hit the Peg again in the next stroke. When a Free Ball or Alive Ball roquets an opponent's ball it makes that ball dead, and robs it of its score of any figure below ten. Each player is responsible for his own score, and must declare it when asked. As soon as a player has a score of ten he is so far safe, and this applies to each ten. The player who first reaches forty, or any other agreed figure, wins the game. Points are not made in any order. A player, when his turn comes, may go for the Peg, or try to run any hoop, but not twice in the same turn consecutively.

The following Definitions are important:—

ROQUET.—Making a roquet gives the right to another turn, and any score belonging to the roqueted ball under ten, between ten and twenty, between twenty and thirty, or between thirty and forty is robbed from the roqueted ball, and placed to the credit of the Striker making the roquet. The roqueted ball is killed, and must start again from Baulk A, and must make the First Hoop before becoming again a Free Ball.

DEAD BALL.—All the balls are dead at the beginning of the game, and must be played from Baulk A. No ball can score until, having made the First Hoop it becomes a Free Ball.

AN ALIVE BALL.—Is a free ball that has scored.

The Laws of Polo (or Robber) Croquet are not contained in the Law Book published by the Croquet Association, but a copy of them can be obtained on application to the Croquet Association Office.

III
MALLETS

A good Croquet mallet has certain essential characteristics: —
(1) It must be well balanced for the style of the player.
(2) The hole through the head for the shaft must be accurately bored.
(3) The shaft must be straight.
(4) The grip must be set correctly into the head.
(5) The grain in the shaft should either be exactly at right-angles to the head—which is preferable—or exactly parallel to it, not anyhow!

(1) Balance depends on the relative weights of head and shaft. Some players like all the weight in the head, others like a more even balance. To find whether a mallet is well balanced for *you* try whether, when you begin to draw it back for your stroke, it responds at once from the head. If there is a sort of reluctance about it and you have, as it were, to drag it back, then whatever merits it may have it is not well balanced for *you*.

With the question of balance, of course, comes in the matter of weight. Years ago the tendency was towards heavy mallets. The standard Corbally Mallet weighed 3 lbs. 9 ozs. Most players to-day would regard this as over-heavy, and there is a school of players who go in for extremely light mallets well under 3 lbs.

Players do not always realise that weight and timing are intimately connected. A light pendulum will swing quickly, a heavy pendulum slowly. If you have a heavy mallet you must time your stroke slowly; if you have a light mallet you can time your stroke more quickly.

A player sometimes wonders why, when he was playing so well in practice, he is not playing equally well in his tournament game. The answer is almost always just this: that under stress of nerves he has quickened his timing, and his mallet, which was quite correct for his practice timing, is too heavy for his tournament timing. If you are inclined to stick in easy hoops for no very obvious cause, you can be pretty sure that your mallet is too heavy for your timing. You must either time more slowly—not always easy—or have a lighter mallet.

We come then to this conclusion. The weight of the mallet must be adequate to do its job, but not too heavy for the timing of the player.

We would suggest to the beginner that if a Centre Player his or her mallet should weigh 3 lbs. to 3 lbs. 8 ozs. 3 lbs. 5 ozs. is an excellent weight; if a Side Player, about 3 lbs. to 3 lbs. 2 ozs.

It should, however, be added that there are many players who are very successful with the extremely light Australian type of mallet, in which the lack of weight in the head is compensated for by the elasticity of the supple cane shaft. Perhaps later on these mallets will once more become obtainable, but at the moment of writing they are not to be had. As to the usual type of English mallet, with hickory shaft and lignum vitae or boxwood head, the weights above suggested are strongly recommended.

Under the head of balance comes also the question of the length of the shaft. This is mainly a matter of taste. You won't get very far unless you feel thoroughly comfortable, therefore let your mallet shaft be of a length that is most comfortable for you. Broadly speaking, shortness gives freedom and length steadiness. Over-short mallets are apt to be unsteady, therefore there is no object in having your mallet shorter than is necessary for comfort and freedom.

(3) That the shaft should be straight seems to be too obvious to require emphasis. Unfortunately hickory, of which most shafts are made, though ideal for the purpose in many respects, has a great tendency to warp. Therefore, in buying a mallet take careful note of the straightness of the shaft and, to say the least, get a mallet with as straight a shaft as you possibly can!

(4) Again, it is obvious that the grip must be set accurately with the head. But this is by no means always found to be the case in fact. Often players are puzzled because they keep missing one side or the other, and the fault is not the

MALLETS

predominance referred to elsewhere but just that the grip of the shaft is not true with the head.

By the by, while mentioning the setting of the grip with the head, it may be remarked that many players—especially Centre Players—find it more comfortable to have the grip wider sideways, so to speak, than back to front in the old way.

(5) The reason why the grain of the hickory of the shaft should be either at right angles to the head, or exactly parallel, is not so obvious as the other essential requirements. When the grain is at right angles with the head a good drive is obtained, and even if the shaft slightly warps the "lean" will not be so disastrous as it would be sideways. If, on the other hand, the grain is exactly parallel the drive is even better, but, of course, any warp will be completely destructive. Therefore we advise that to have the grain at right angles is the better way; but to have it parallel has some advantages. But to have it anyhow is to be avoided, as having the advantages of neither method, and having a disadvantage of its own in being likely to swing out of the straight.

The foregoing are the essentials—here are a few mallet details entirely within the sphere of individual choice.

Many different grips are used to give a good hold and keep the hands from slipping. Some shafts are bound with string, some with cork, some with golf-grips. Cork is soft and pleasant to the touch, and can be kept in good condition by the occasional use of a sponge and cold water. Many players, however, prefer just to have the plain wood milled.

Most mallets have octagon grips, but a few have oval grips; these latter are mostly of cork and used to be very popular, especially with shafts of malacca cane.

Most mallet shafts are made of hickory, and probably, take it all round, nothing can be much better. Steel golf-shafts have some advantages, but have not gained much popularity so far. Malacca cane is also used, and the Australian malia cane was becoming very popular before the war but for the moment, at any rate, is unobtainable.

MALLETS

Mallet heads are of lignum vitae and boxwood. In these days lignum is the more popular. It is a very heavy wood, very resilient but also somewhat brittle, so that a lignum head is best brass-bound. Box is rather lighter, but less brittle and less resilient. It does not require to be brass-bound.

With regard to the "springiness" of hickory mallet shafts: a stiff, steely spring is excellent for the Stop Shot and Long Shooting, but not good for Hoop-running and Roll Strokes. A supple, whippy shaft is good for Hoop-running and Roll Strokes but not for Stop Shots and Long Shooting. It is better, therefore, to take a middle course and have a moderately whippy shaft.

Owing to its lightness the Australian cane-shafted mallet is very good for Stop Shots, and because of its supple shaft it is also good for Rolls and Hoop-running.

In ordering a mallet from Messrs. Jaques, or any other maker, care should be taken to specify the exact length of the shaft, stating clearly whether the length given includes the head or not; the length and thickness of the grip and, of course, the weight. Unless ordered otherwise, heads are usually about 9 inches long and just under 3 inches in diameter. The diameter of the head may, however, be reduced to $2\frac{3}{4}$ inches, or even $2\frac{5}{8}$ inches. Indeed, this is often necessary in cases where the full-sized head would come out too heavy. Most heads are round, but some are square and some cut away at the sides. This is all a matter of individual taste.

In conclusion, we would stress the extreme importance of the five requirements mentioned at the beginning of this chapter, and also that a player must feel thoroughly comfortable with his or her mallet.

STYLE

It is important that a decision as to which style to adopt should be made as soon as possible, and then adhered to.

Though there is much scope for individual taste in matters of detail, Croquet styles fall under three main groups:—
1. "Playing between the feet," called the "Irish style" or, more usually now, CENTRE PLAY. 2. Facing the object ball as in Centre Play, but actuating the mallet at the side of either foot, SIDE PLAY. 3. Using the mallet somewhat like a golf club or cricket bat and swinging across the body. As this is unquestionably the original and oldest style we will call it the OLD STYLE.

1. CENTRE PLAY.—This style has one great advantage. The mallet is swung pendulum fashion directly in the line of aim. Diagrams 1 and 2 show the usual positions for feet, mallet and ball. Some players have both feet level, as in Diagram 1; others put one foot forward, as in Diagram 2. If the mallet is gripped high on the shaft the tendency will be to have both feet level; if the shaft is gripped lower it will be natural and comfortable to advance one foot or the other. As to the height of the hands on the shaft, hold the shaft as low as you *must* and as high as you *can*. As low as you must for accuracy and confidence, as high as you can to avoid fatigue.

The GRIP is important. Take hold of the shaft with the left hand, with the thumb in front pointing downwards. Then place the right hand on the shaft with the little finger overlapping the first finger of the left hand. *Vice versa*, of course, if you are left-handed. It is a matter for individual preference as to whether the little finger of the right hand just touches the shaft or not.

Though the above is the standard grip, we must add that the hands may be placed one above the other without any overlap; indeed, one first-class player has them widely separated. And some players, especially those who separate the hands for some or all strokes, place the upper hand the reverse way, with knuckles in front, and thumb behind, as in Side Play.

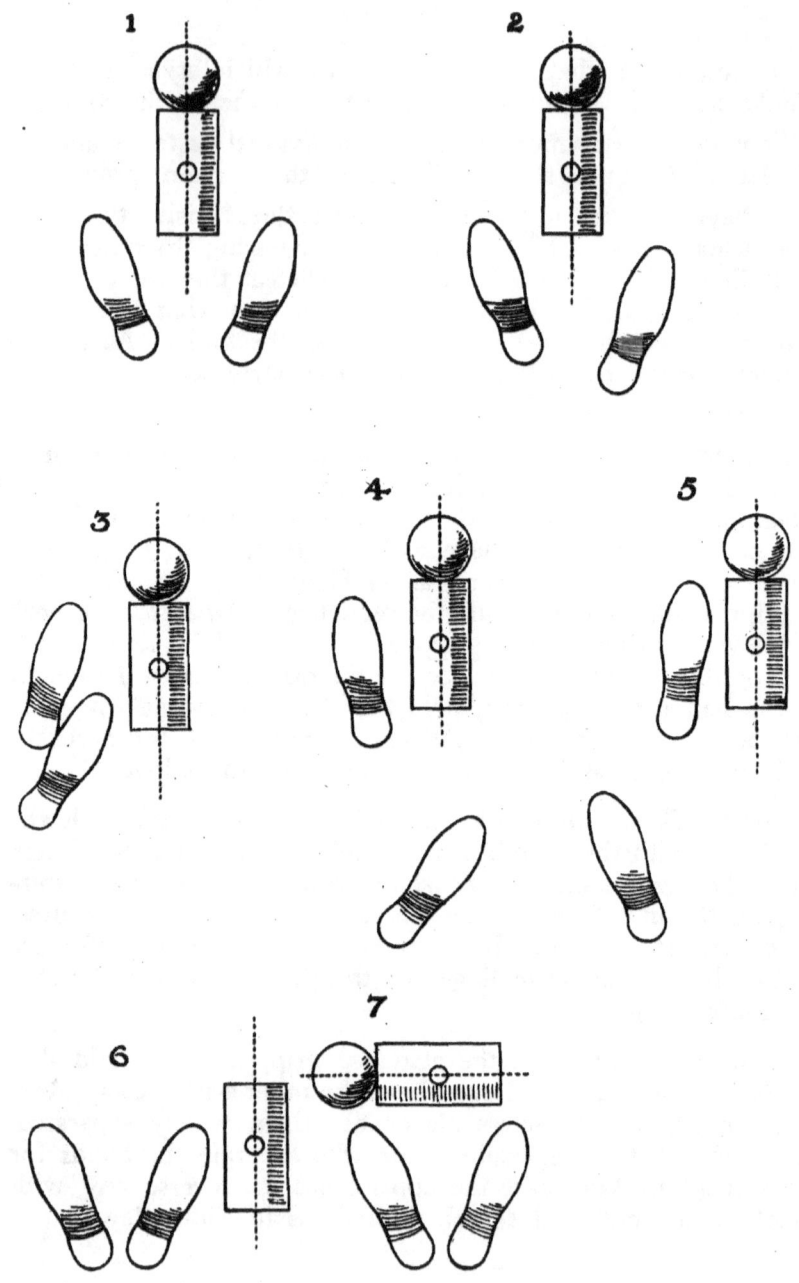

STYLE

Hands vary in size, fingers in length, so that in the last resort each player must work out his or her own best grip. Comfort, by the by, is essential. No player is going to do much good if there is a feeling that grip, or stance, is unnatural or uncomfortable.

There is one fault the Centre-Player must look out for, and that is Hand- or Foot-predominance. If you are inclined to keep on missing on the Left, you are suffering from Right-predominance; if on the Right, from Left-predominance.

If there is predominance either left or right there are three things to be looked to: your grip may need adjustment; one hand or the other may be exercising too much pressure; the mallet shaft may be too thin or too thick. Most likely of all, your stance may need correcting. If the trouble is Right-predominance, causing you to keep missing on the left, bring the Right Foot further forward and take the Left further back. *Vice versa* if the trouble is Left-predominance. Please take special note of the fact that whereas the player you are playing against is only a friendly opponent, predominance left or right is a most bitter enemy and must be ruthlessly fought against.

2. SIDE PLAY.—In this style, as in Centre Play, the aim is straight and natural, but the mallet is swung at the side of one or other foot. This necessitates the bending of head and body and very considerable care to get a good balance. Diagrams 3-6 give the usual feet, mallet and ball positions for this style.

With regard to the grip, the left hand is placed near the top of the shaft, with the thumb either on the top or just behind. The right hand is placed some distance down in the reverse position. As to the placing of the right hand, there is considerable variation among Side Players. Some bring it near the left hand, others have it far down the shaft.

Like the Centre Player, the Side Player has to fight ruthlessly against hand- or foot- predominance. If a right-handed player, he or she is almost certain to suffer at times from right-predominance, which is likely to manifest itself in causing the mallet to swing round the body instead of straight out towards the object ball.

If you find that you are suffering from predominance you must consider just the same things as the Centre Player in like case. But whereas his trouble is most likely to be something wrong with the position of his feet, yours as a Side Player is most likely to be something wrong with the position of the hands, especially with the right hand. The right hand may be too far round the shaft, or not far enough.

Also be specially careful of the stroke itself. Take every possible care that the mallet should swing out directly towards the object ball, and not come round the body. This swinging-round-the-body is the special danger of Side Play and must be carefully guarded against.

It need hardly be said that in the case of a left-handed player the above directions and suggestions must be reversed accordingly.

3. THE OLD STYLE.—In this style the mallet is swung across the body from right to left, like a cricket bat or golf club. A book on Croquet would not be complete without mentioning it, because there are at least two excellent players who still use it with great effect. But, frankly, it is not a style to be recommended to the beginner, because any advantage in the matter of control is so completely outweighed by the greater difficulty of aiming. Diagram 7 gives the usual feet, mallet and ball positions for the Old Style.

Which style should the beginner adopt? In view of the remarks already made as to the Old Style, this question resolves itself into the problem of Centre Play *versus* Side Play.

In view of the fact that both these styles have always numbered and do still number among their adherents players at "the very top of the tree," it is not an altogether easy matter to decide.

Centre Play is probably easier to learn, because of its absolutely direct aim and pendulum-like swing in the line of aim. To become proficient with it, however, does require much suppleness of wrist, not possessed by everyone; and, of course, it is the more tiring of the two styles.

STYLE

Side Play is more difficult to learn. With it a satisfactory stance and a good free swing out to the object ball are definitely more troublesome to acquire. But perseverance does overcome these difficulties.

Any idea that Centre Play is the only proper style for men and Side Play the only proper style for women is ridiculous, in view of the many splendid men players who have used, and do use, Side Play; and the excellent women players, both at home and many more beyond the seas, who have used, and do use, Centre Play. Moreover, we live in an age of " sports clothes," not of crinolines!

Before dismissing the whole subject of styles we would remark that it is a curious feature of our game that the style, even including details of grip and stance, that a player adopts as a raw recruit is often retained throughout his or her Croquet career. The obvious moral is that all the greater care should be taken to make the right choice at the beginning.

DIAGRAM 1. HITTING TRUE.

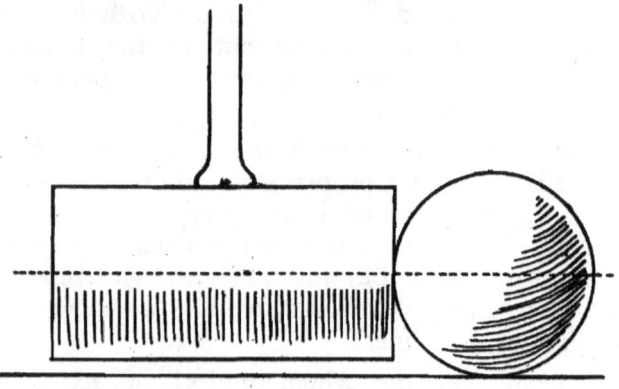

DIAGRAM 2. HITTING DOWN.

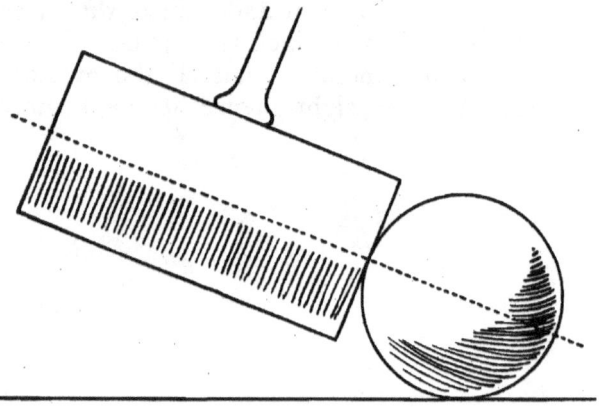

DIAGRAM 3. HITTING UP.

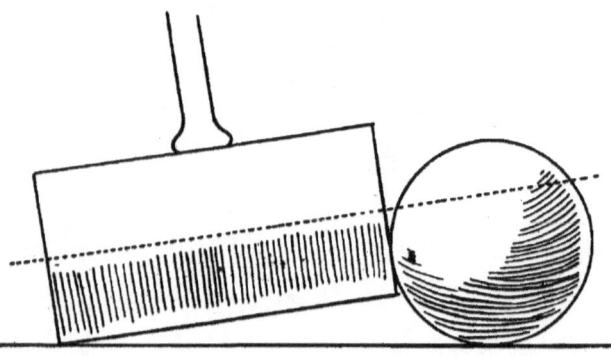

V

HITTING ONE'S OWN BALL

A GREAT authority on Croquet has laid it down that there is only one really difficult thing in the game, and that is to hit one's own ball in the correct way.

Here are seven important rules to remember: —

(1) Previous to aiming, "stalk your ball"—that is, walk up to it in the line of aim.

(2) When aiming, being a Centre or Side Player, fairly and squarely face the direction of aim.

(3) As regards hands, wrists and arms, hold your mallet firmly, taking care of the placing of your fingers; let your wrists be reasonably flexible—especially for Centre Play; keep your arms in.

(4) During the stroke keep your head and body as still as possible.

(5) In beginning the back swing of the mallet take care that the mallet begins to move back from the toe of the head pendulum fashion, not from the top of the shaft. If you are a Centre Player, press with your thumbs to achieve this result.

(6) Having taken aim, keep your eyes glued to the back of your own ball until it is well on its way. The act of looking up during the stroke throws out the swing of the mallet, and is very often fatal.

(7) Trust your mallet. Having a good mallet and swinging it correctly, let the weight of the mallet do its job. Don't hold it with vice-like grip and tight wrists and try to do all the work yourself by force.

We now come to four different methods of hitting one's own ball, which will be constantly referred to in the following pages: —

(1) Hitting True. (2) Hitting down, or topping. (3) Hitting up. (4) Hitting on the right or left side of the head.

(1) HITTING TRUE.—This method gives the ball the full weight of the mallet, and is the normal method for Roquets and Hoop-running.

Keep the mallet head as close to the ground as you can so that the point of contact with the ball is as near the centre of the face of the mallet-head as possible. In actual fact, it will usually be found that the point of contact is just below the centre of the mallet face, and this for practical purposes may be passed as "good enough," but, nevertheless, when hitting true try your best to hit the ball with the dead centre of your mallet face.

(2) HITTING DOWN, OR TOPPING.—This is the method for all Roll Strokes. It has, of course, the effect of pinching the ball between the mallet head and the ground and so producing an upward line-of-force. The point of contact between mallet head and ball should be about the centre of the mallet head.

(3) HITTING UP.—This is the special method for Stop Shots and other strokes that will be referred to in the following pages. The point of contact between mallet-head and ball should be below the centre of the face of the head—indeed, as near the bottom edge as possible. This method is, of course, the Croquet equivalent of screw in billiards.

(4) HITTING ON THE RIGHT OR LEFT SIDE OF THE MALLET-HEAD.—This method is the Croquet equivalent of side in billiards. Like Hitting Up, it has Stop Shot effect and is useful for some Double Strokes, especially for short Hoop Approaches. The Stop Shot effect can be increased by Hitting Up as well as hitting on the side of the mallet-head. To avoid an unnecessary illustration, think of the face of the mallet-head as the face of a clock with the XII at the top. Then hitting on the side means hitting on the III or the IX, or with greater Stop-effect on the spot just below the IV or the VIII.

It need hardly be said that whereas the possibilities for the use of side in billiards are almost endless, in Croquet they are severely limited.

It must, however, be remarked that whereas Methods 1, 2 and 3 are absolutely essential, Method 4 can be dispensed with, and is, in fact, unused by many first-class players. Nevertheless, for those who care to study it, it is of value for certain special purposes as indicated in the following pages, and no book dealing with the Strokes of the game would be complete without mention of it. But it belongs to "advanced" rather than to "beginner's" Croquet, and beginners would be well advised to let it alone until some proficiency in the game has been attained.

VI

SINGLE STROKES

SINGLE STROKES may be classified as: —
(1) The ROQUET.
(2) The Rush.
(3) Hoop-running.
(4) Playing to a Given Spot.
(5) The Jump.

(1) THE ROQUET.—Consideration of this stroke takes one straight to the paramount question of: How to aim? Any player may safely adopt the following plan: First, from a little distance behind your ball, take a good look at both the object ball and your ball. Then mentally visualize a straight line running through the centres of both balls. Then stalk your ball—that is, walk up to it in an extension of this line—keeping eyes and mind rigidly fixed on the line of aim. Now place your mallet behind your ball exactly in the line of aim. Then withdraw your eyes entirely from the object ball, and concentrate them on the exact spot where the line of aim passes from your mallet-head into your ball. Remember that at all costs you must hit that spot. And remember, too, that however good a player your opponent may be, he can do nothing whatever to prevent you hitting it!

No doubt all this sounds complicated, but you will soon do it unconsciously. If you are not a beginner you probably do it unconsciously already, but you will find a memory of the scheme, step by step, a useful tonic for restoring your confidence, if you have missed a short roquet or two!

As aids to mentally visualizing the all-important line of aim, some players hold the mallet-head for a moment or two above the ball before placing it behind; others take a last and very quick look at the object ball before bringing their eyes back to the all-important spot on their own ball, and striking.

In special connection with the Roquet, careful consideration should be given to the directions in the preceding section on: How to hit your own ball. The method of hitting for the Roquet is to hit true.

DIAGRAM 1.

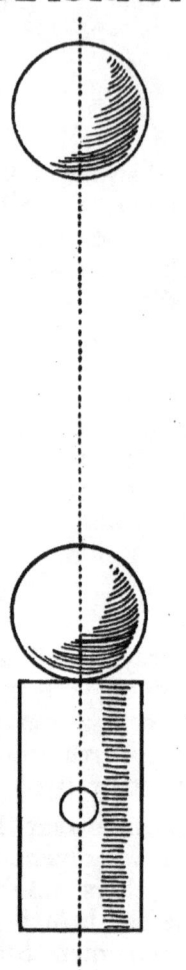

THE ROQUET.

DIAGRAM 2.

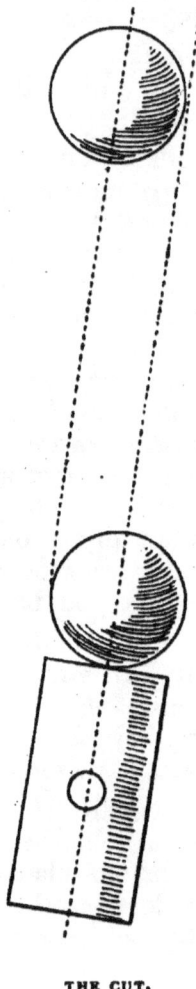

THE CUT.

SINGLE STROKES

WHY ARE SHORT ROQUETS SO OFTEN MISSED?—If you have missed a short roquet—unless you are physically "off colour" and so cannot aim straight, the reason is sure to be (1) Predominance. This has been already dealt with in the Section on Style. (2) Failure to bring the eyes back from the object ball to the all-important spot on your own ball. How often has a player exclaimed, when sudden unexpected disaster has come: "I never even saw my own ball at all!" Or (3), and most likely of the three, looking up in the act of striking. This fault is absolutely deadly and again and again brings sudden catastrophy.

Avoid these faults with all the energy you can, but if you make a slip do not be too down-hearted. Even the super-cracks are tripped up by one or other of these errors every now and then, and have to pay the penalty!

(2) THE RUSH.—This is a Roquet made with intent not only to hit the object ball but to drive it forward a given distance in a given direction.

As to straight Rushes, nothing need be added to what has already been said under the head of The Roquet. As to correct strength, practice alone will bring accuracy. But do not be satisfied with "anything will do"; always note, and have a good look at the spot to which you wish to drive the object ball, and persistently try to get it there.

On a good lawn the method of hitting is to hit true; but if the lawn is in the least rough it is wise to hit up. Hitting up is a precaution against jumping. Even if your ball does not leap right over the object ball, but merely jumps and hits it above the centre, your Rush will be ruined. To hit down even to the smallest extent is completely fatal.

When it is desired to rush the object ball out of the straight, the stroke is called a Cut Rush, or more briefly a Cut.

The Cut differs from the straight rush only in the matter of aiming. In aiming you must try to visualize a straight line on the right side of your own ball if you are cutting to the right, to the left if you are cutting to the left, and this line must pass through the object ball with a reasonable margin of safety. A glance at the diagram will make the matter quite clear.

SINGLE STROKES

It is hardly wise to try to cut at a greater distance than about a yard!

(3) HOOP-RUNNING.—The great difference between running a hoop and making a roquet is that whereas in the latter case you are aiming at a solid object, in the former you are aiming at a space. This distinction is important. When players have an attack of "hoopitis" the trouble is quite likely to be that their thoughts are concentrated on the Hoop Uprights and not on the space between them. Remember that it is the space between the iron Uprights of the Hoop that must have your attention, not the Uprights themselves!

In aiming, try to visualize a spot in the very centre of the space between the Uprights, and aim directly towards it.

When, however, your position is very sideways, you have to try and visualize parallel straight lines, one passing the side of your ball and just clearing the nearer Upright of the Hoop, and the other going through the centre of your ball and inside the further Upright.

To decide whether a hoop is reasonably possible, divide your ball mentally into three parts, and unless two of them will seemingly pass comfortably within the further Upright, do not attempt it. It may be remarked, however, that in desperate situations hoops that appear impossible are sometimes run.

There is one special method for running hoops that is worth mentioning. It might be called the method of Direct Aim. The mallet-head, instead of being placed behind the ball, is placed above the ball. The player then visualizes two straight lines, one on each side of the mallet-head, passing through the hoop equidistant from each Upright. He then allows the mallet to fall slowly back, dropping into position as it goes, and strikes straight away. This method is worth noting, because even if it is not adopted as a permanent part of one's game it can be brought into temporary use as a cure for "hoopitis."

The ordinary methods for hitting the ball in Hoop-running are as follows:—

(a) If you are in good position for your hoop, and can afford to run through at a moderate pace, hit true, putting the smallest

SINGLE STROKES

amount of lift into your stroke; *i.e.*, when the mallet-head strikes the ball let it be just a trifle more on the rise than it would be for an ordinary roquet.

(b) If you are in good position, but need to run the hoop specially slowly, keep the mallet-head as close to the ground as possible, and use a slow sweeping stroke without any lift in it, striking the ball as much above the centre of the face of your mallet-head as you possibly can. You will be surprised at the hoops that you can run quite slowly, even from a distance, by this method.

(c) If you are in a sideways position hit up with a sharp, firm stroke. If you are near the hoop you can check the heel of the mallet-head on the ground to prevent a foul.

An alternative method that some players are very successful with is to hit down on to the ball, so that it jumps, tends to climb the hoop upright and fall through.

(d) If you are at the side, and very near the hoop, raise your mallet from the ground quite evenly and strike your ball as though it was a large egg and you were trying to cut the top of it off at one stroke. There are plenty of cases when this is the only method that is likely to succeed.

There are three golden rules for the stroke in Hoop-running. There must be no jerk at the beginning of the back-swing. The stroke must not be hurried. The mallet must have time to swing. If you are a Centre Player be specially careful, with the objects in view, to keep your wrists flexible. These rules, which are important for all Single Strokes, are specially so for Hoop-running.

In order to avoid the fatal jerk at the beginning of the back-swing it often pays not to ground the mallet at all for Hoop-running.

Either or both, the fatal jerk and the quick back-swing utterly destroy the sweet, smooth stroke that is essential for good Hoop-running. Specially for Hoop-running: *Take care of the back-swing and the front-swing will take care of itself.*

(4) PLAYING TO A GIVEN SPOT.—The only direction that it is necessary to give for this stroke is: Look well at the spot

STANDARD SETTING.

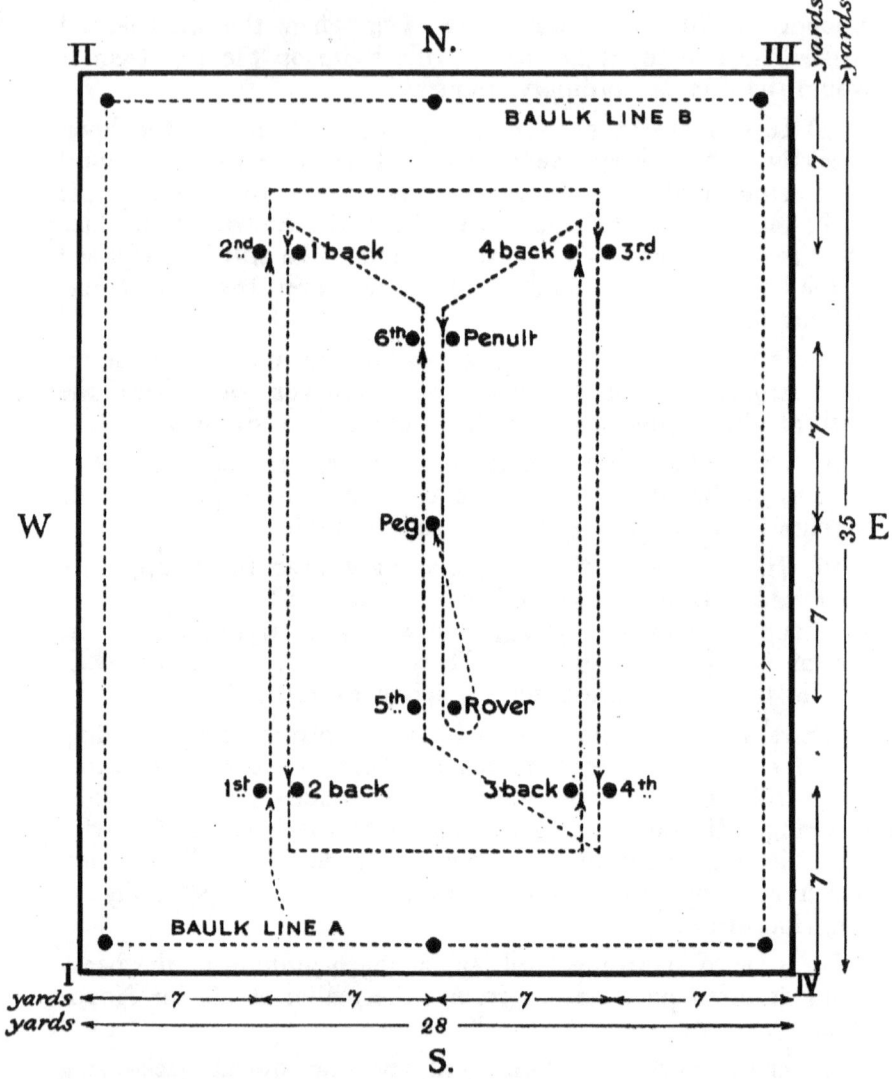

Only those portions indicated by a continuous line need be marked on the court.

The order of making the points is indicated by the arrows.

For the dimensions of the modified court setting see Law 2 (b).

you want to put your ball on before aiming and striking. If you register the spot in your mind, there is a strong chance that you may get there. It is no exaggeration to say that the difference between sending a ball 2ft. and 2ft. 6ins. may be the difference between winning and losing a game; therefore, do not be satisfied with the thought that anywhere more or less near the chosen spot will do.

(5) THE JUMP.—This stroke comes in if you get "stymied" from the object ball, or the Peg, or blocked by another ball in a hoop. Aim carefully, and then hit down hard on to the top of your ball.

If it is desirable that the ball blocking a hoop should go through as well as yours (if, for example, you have failed in a peel) this can be achieved by not over-doing the hitting down, so that your ball instead of making a clean jump, mounts the back of the obstructing ball and both go through. This is a useful stroke and well worth some practice. As, however, it is a stroke rather apt to cause a hole in the ground, it would be well to practice it on some odd piece of ground and not on the Croquet Court itself.

Before leaving the subject of Single Strokes, we would emphasize the fact that all Croquet Strokes, and especially the Single Strokes, depend on timing and rhythm. Each stroke must be a smooth pendulum swing from start to finish. When, for example, a player begins his stroke by pulling the mallet back with a jerk, he is committing a fault in timing that is utterly destructive to the rhythm. To avoid this fault the advice is often given—and it is good advice—" Slowly back! " But "Slowly back" is only a virtue if it means avoiding the fatal jerk, and having the whole stroke unified and rhythmic. There is no virtue at all in taking the mallet slowly back and then jerking it forward! Even when a player has to hit hard it should not be a matter of brute force, but only of an extra free rhythmic swing. Always be specially careful of the back-swing. There must be no jerk at the beginning of it, and no jerk forward at the end of it. Let the mallet go back as far as it seems to want to. Give the mallet time to swing.

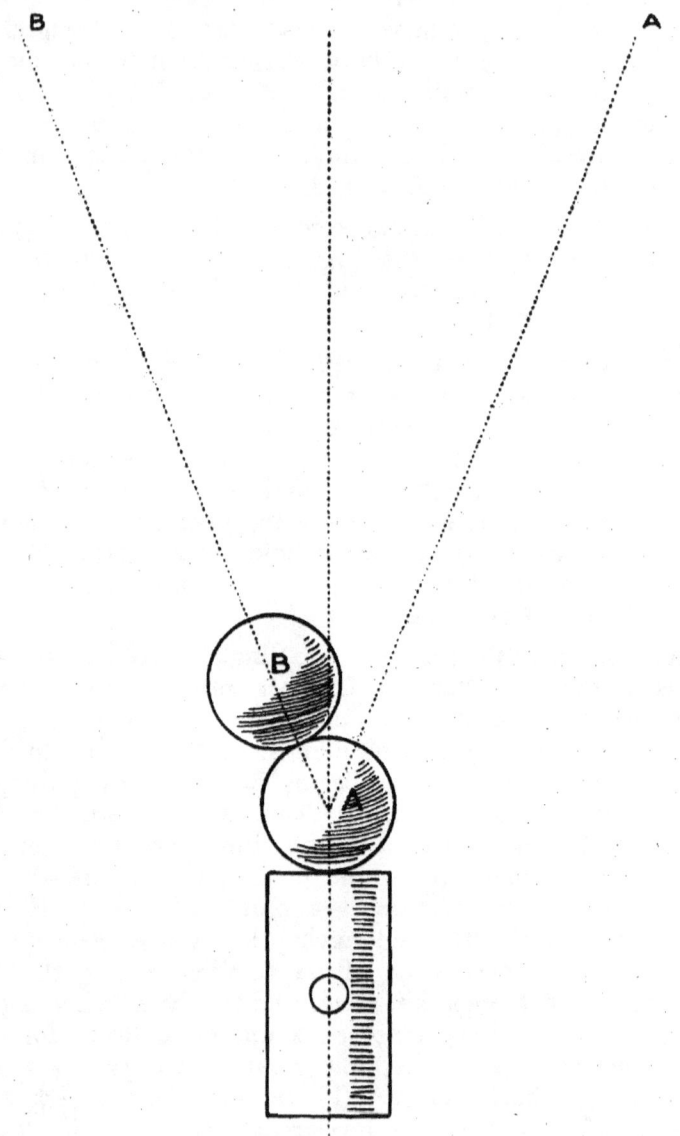

The aim for a split stroke.

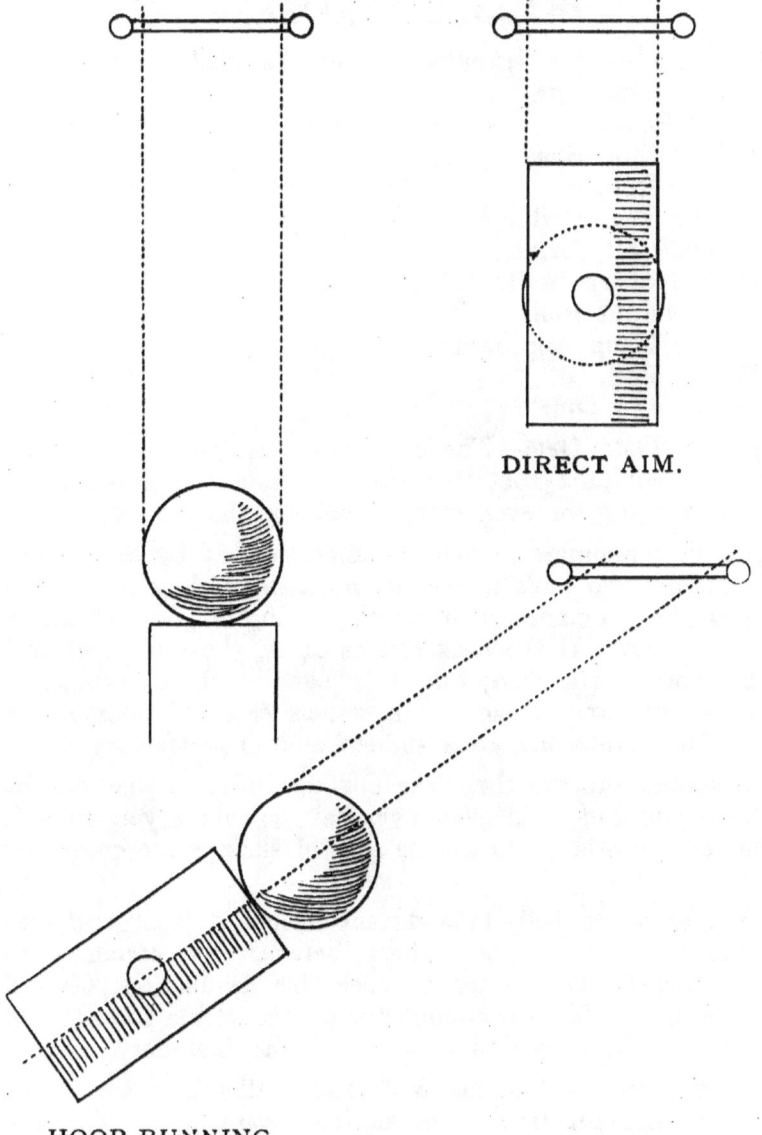

DIRECT AIM.

HOOP RUNNING.

DOUBLE STROKES

DOUBLE or CROQUET STROKES may be classified as follows:—
(1) The Take Off.
(2) The Drive.
(3) The Stop Shot.
(4) The Roll.
(5) The Pass Roll.
(6) The Split Drive.
(7) The Sharp Split.
(8) The Split Roll.
(10) The Hoop Approach.
(11) The Peel.
(12) The Peg Out.

(1) THE TAKE OFF.—The object of this stroke is to send your own ball to a spot that may be distant or near, while only just moving, or even merely shaking, the croqueted ball.

The rule for aiming is that the angle formed by the mallet-head and the two balls in contact must be slightly more than a right angle. A glance at the accompanying diagram will make this quite clear. If the striker aims at A, the croqueted ball will be moved or shaken; but if he aims at B, the croqueted ball may not even shake. (In which case, of course, the striker's turn will come to a sudden and unsatisfactory end!)

You should practise the Take Off carefully, so that on the one hand you can make your own ball go where you want it to, and on the other, you can be sure of shaking the croqueted ball.

In taking off to balls in a distant corner, it is a good idea to concentrate on a spot midway between the corner hoop and the corner. If you try to reach this destination you will be pretty sure to be near enough for a comfortable roquet; and you are not likely to find yourself off the boundary.

(2) THE DRIVE.—Let the balls and mallet-head be in the same line, and hit true. The desired result is to send the croqueted ball about two-thirds as far again as your own ball. The Drive should be a perfectly natural stroke without any assistance from hitting up or hitting down, etc. The Drive

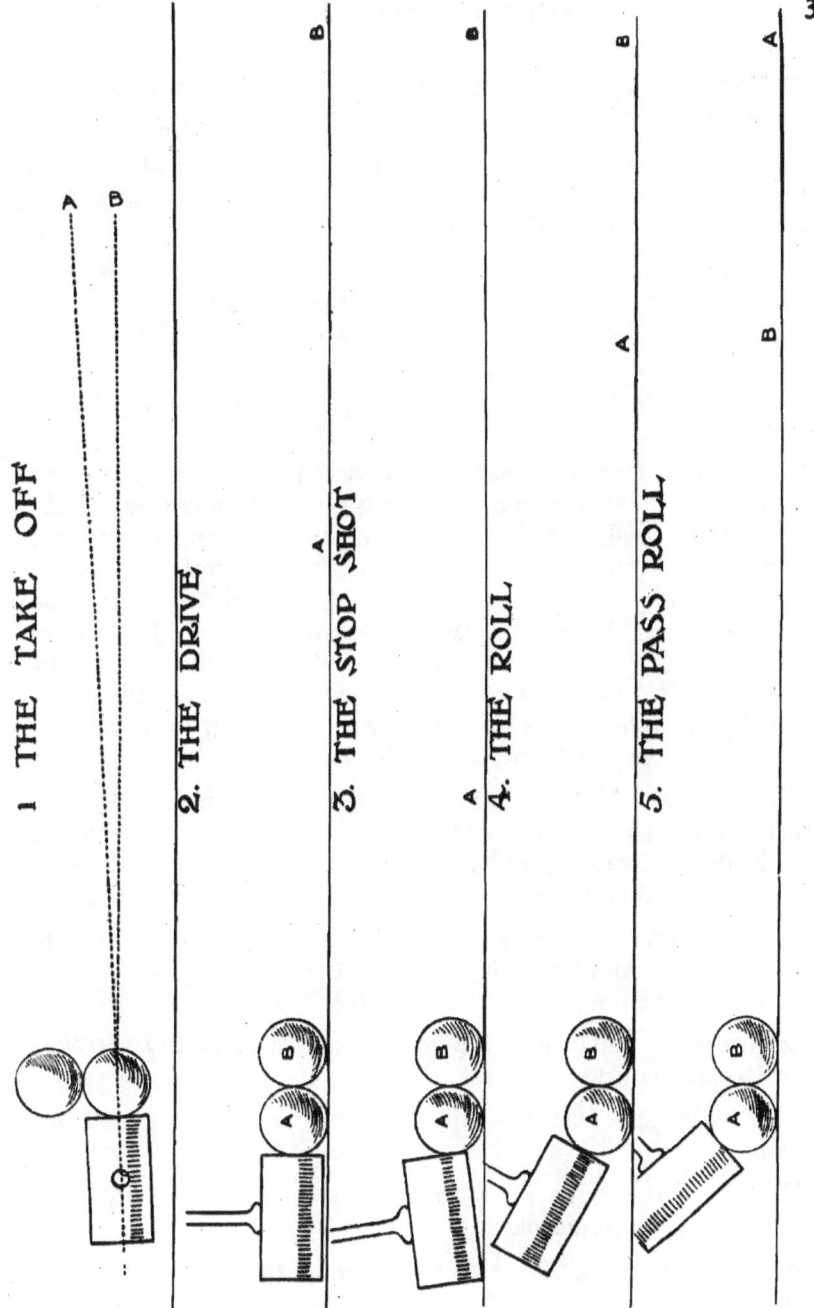

is the special stroke for trying out what your mallet will do for you, with hitting true, and an ordinary swing.

(3) THE STOP SHOT.—Aim as for the Drive, but hit up. The desired result is to send the croqueted ball a long way and your own ball only a short way.

(4) THE ROLL.—Again have balls and mallet-head in line, but this time hit down, putting steady pressure in your stroke. If you are a Centre Player slip your hands lower down the shaft, and, as a matter of fact, if you are a Side Player do the same, or at least put your lower hand further down the shaft.

Be it specially noted that hitting down for rolls, even very short ones, is most important. If you try to do them by merely pushing you are almost certain to make a foul. Your opponent, acting possibly on a "knock for knock" basis, may not claim it, and, indeed, a slight amount of "give and take" in this matter is desirable because an unevenness in the lawn may cause a perfectly fair stroke to become a technical foul; but the limits of toleration are *quickly reached,* and if you habitually offend by audible rattles you will deservedly run into trouble. Therefore be sure and hit down for rolls.

(5) THE PASS ROLL.—Aim as before, but hit more down still, and put the hands lower still. The Pass Roll stroke is a really difficult stroke, and in play, but not in practice, should as far as possible be avoided.

SPLIT STROKES.—The rule for aiming in all Split Strokes is as follows: Aim midway between the points to which the balls are respectively intended to travel.

Remembering this rule, the names of the next four strokes are self-explanatory.

(6) THE SPLIT DRIVE.—Hit true, but aim as for a Split Stroke.

(7) THE SHARP SPLIT or SPLIT STOP SHOT.—Hit up, but aim as for a Split Stroke.

(8) THE SPLIT ROLL.—Hit down, and again aim as for a Split Stroke.

DOUBLE STROKES

(9) THE SPLIT PASS ROLL.—Hit down, only more so, and aim as for a Split Stroke. The wider the split, the easier this stroke will become.

Important Notes

(1) In Split Strokes Croquet balls have a tendency to pull in, and this must be allowed for. This pull in is reduced to a minimum in strokes of Stop Shot type, and is much stronger in all Roll Strokes.

(2) In actual play the Double Strokes that have been mentioned tend to merge into one another with an infinite number of gradations, but in all these strokes the following rules will hold true:—

(a) If you hit true the croqueted ball will go about two-thirds as far again as your own ball, except that the wider the split the less will be the difference of travel between the two balls.

(b) If you hit up you will increase the distance of travel of the croqueted ball, and decrease that of your own ball.

(c) If you hit down you will increase the distance of travel of your own ball as compared to that of the croqueted ball.

The foregoing are the Standard Croquet Strokes; the three following are really applications of these to special purposes.

10. THE APPROACH.—As far as possible by accurate rushing seek to be able to approach your hoops with miniature Stop Shots or Drives from right in front. Avoid as much as you can having to use Rolls for hoop approaching, because these are most dangerous.

In approaching hoops, if you care to try and use it, you may find Side of value. If you are approaching a hoop from, say, three feet away, and you are slightly on the left, use the right side of the face of your mallet-head. This is less jerky than the ordinary hitting up Stop Shot method, but also takes the weight of the mallet-head off the ball, and so lessens the chance of over-running the hoop. If you are on the left, use the left side of the face of your mallet-head.

DOUBLE STROKES

This use of Side is difficult to describe on paper, but if you try it in practice you will find it extremely useful for approaching hoops, and as you become accustomed to it you will find other opportunities of bringing it to your aid.

But Side is not essential, and if you feel that it would be merely an additional complication you can cut it out.

A stroke that is always rather frightening is the Take Off Approach from the wrong side of the hoop. This stroke is not nearly as difficult as it looks. But you must run your ball close to the Hoop Upright; indeed, it is often best to aim directly at the Upright.

A special beginner's error is to forget that the Split Stroke rule applies as much to small Splits in approaching hoops as to large ones. When approaching a hoop, therefore, instead of aiming midway between the points to which he wishes the balls to travel, he aims directly at the spot in front of the hoop to which he wishes his ball to go. The result is, of course, disaster!

When you have to use a Roll Stroke for an approach, be specially careful not to over-roll it. After all, if you are not quite far enough you may be able to try to run the hoop, but if you have over-rolled it you are done!

By the by, be specially careful in your approach strokes that the two balls are securely touching. Many a first-class player playing splendid Croquet has been deprived of his reward by not noticing, or noticing too late, that the balls were not touching. When the balls are not touching you are almost certain to over-roll the hoop.

When playing a break always remember that it is easier to approach a hoop from a considerable distance right in front than from a much shorter distance from the side. The reason, of course, is that there is a greater margin of error.

If you watch a first-class player you will observe that again and again, almost with monotonous regularity, his ball is about one foot from his hoop right in front. How deceptively easy this looks! But how very difficult it is in practice; nevertheless, it is what the beginner must make it his or her object to achieve.

DOUBLE STROKES

11. THE PEEL.—The object of this stroke is to drive the croqueted ball, and sometimes both balls together, through a hoop.

The first case to be considered is when your own ball is intended to run the hoop in the next stroke.

If you are near the hoop and in good position for peeling, place the balls with the utmost care; look for parallel lines one on each side of the balls passing between the Hoop Uprights, then use the Stop Shot—*i.e.*, hit up.

When the balls are very close to the hoop you can use the Drive—*i.e.*, hit true—or even the Roll and put both balls through together. If your own ball sits in the hoop it does not matter, as you can go through in the next stroke.

If you should have to aim a Peel from a sideways position be specially careful about the croqueted ball clearing the near Hoop Upright.

The second case is when it is not intended to send your own ball through in the next stroke. This often happens in the Triple Peels, when the croqueted ball is being peeled through 4 Back, and the Penultimate, and even the Rover Hoop; and, of course, in the Double Peel for the last two of these.

You carefully manœuvre the ball to be peeled in front of its hoop, probably using it for your own hoop-approach; then when you have run the hoop (in the case of peeling a ball through 4 Back in the Triple Peel you would be running your Third Hoop) you would do the Peel with a short Drive, Stop Shot or Split Roll.

CAUTION.—If you use a Split Stroke for peeling you must be careful to allow for the inward pull. Probably a Roll Stroke is the best for the purpose, because it is likely to impart more follow to the croqueted ball.

12. THE PEG OUT.—There are few things more disappointing to a player than to lose a game at the very end; therefore the Peg Out should receive special consideration.

In aiming, visualize a line running through the centre of the ball to be croqueted and the centre of the Peg. Place your ball behind the ball to be croqueted in an extension of this line. Now test your aim by trying to visualize two parallel lines touching the sides of both balls and passing the Peg at equal distances on each side. If you find that the ball to be croqueted is overlapping you must correct the position of your own ball. If there is no overlap your ball has been correctly placed.

Let your stroke be firm and steady. Preferably hit true, but you may have to use a roll if you are far away, because it is essential that your own ball should be close to the Peg ready to be pegged out in the next stroke without any nervous moment!

If you should be pegging out an opponent's ball hit up, as this will prevent your own ball running on to the Peg.

Do not be too hasty in coming to the conclusion that you are too far from the Peg to peg out safely. It is surprising what long peg outs can be successfully accomplished, provided great care is taken in setting your ball, in your own aim and in the use of an absolutely firm, steady stroke.

Should you be trying to peg out a ball, and to go elsewhere with your own ball—to separate the enemy, for example, in case of failure in the peg out—you must, of course, take great care in allowing for the pull in.

CAUTION.—When you are taking croquet, and especially in hoop approach strokes as already indicated, and in peg outs, be careful that the balls are in contact. Should there be the slightest gap between the ball to be croqueted and your own ball all your efforts are likely to be in vain, and anything may happen. Also in Double Strokes, as well as Single Strokes, *be careful* of your timing and rhythm, and to avoid jerks. The only stroke in which something in the nature of a jerk is perhaps permissible is the Stop Shot.

VIII

BREAK MAKING
(Introductory)

THERE are three methods of making breaks known to Croquet players, the Four Ball Break, the Three Ball Break, and the Two Ball Break.

In the Four Ball Break you have your own ball and three assistant balls. Two of these you use alternately to make the points with, and the third as a stepping-stone between them.

In the Three Ball Break you have your own ball and two assistant balls, which you use alternately to make the points with.

In the Two Ball Break you have your own ball and one assistant ball, with which you make as many points as you can!

Now before we proceed to explain the methods of break making, here are five definitions that we must be quite clear about: —

(a) THE PIONEER BALL.—This is the ball that you send on to the next-hoop-but-one to await your arrival there.

(b) THE MIDDLE BALL.—This is the third assistant ball in the Four Ball Break, that you use as a stepping-stone on your way to the Pioneer Ball that is awaiting you at the next hoop, and in various other ways.

(c) THE RUSH LINE.—This is an imaginary line running through the centre of the Pioneer Ball and the hoop to which it has been sent, and the extension of it. Or it may run through the centres of two balls, or through a ball and the Peg. See the accompanying diagrams on Pages 52 and 53.

(d) The Approach (already dealt with) is the Croquet Stroke immediately before the attempt to run a hoop. It is the position-gaining stroke.

(e) THE PRELIMINARY APPROACH.—This is the Croquet Stroke immediately before roqueting the Pioneer Ball at a hoop.

Now if you make quite sure, by reading them over two or three times, that these definitions are well in your mind, it will make what follows much easier to understand.

Obviously the Four Ball Break with its comfortable stepping-stone is the easiest method of break making; therefore, of course, you will seek to use it whenever possible. The next best thing is the Three Ball Break, which, though more difficult, is quite reliable when played correctly. The Two Ball Break you will avoid as much as you can; but it is often useful for snatching two or three points out of a difficult situation, especially the last two or three points before pegging out.

These Breaks have been and can be described at great length and with many diagrams illustrating the positions all the way round the lawn. We shall seek, however, to combine brevity with clearness, and for this reason we shall omit the small strokes round the hoops. For example, the simple statement, " Blue makes the First Hoop off Red," will mean " Blue rushes Red to a spot close in front of the First Hoop, takes croquet off Red, sending it beyond the hoop, and taking position (the Approach), then runs the hoop, then roquets Red again."

Our method of explaining the Breaks will be to set down in sections *what has to be done*, followed by explanations and advice as to *how to do it*.

IX

THE FOUR BALL BREAK

WE will start from a prepared position as follows: Place Blue at A with a rush on Yellow towards C. Place Black at C, and Red at B.

Blue rushes Yellow to a spot about three yards short of Black, then croquets it to D, going himself near Black. Blue roquets Black, then croquets it, leaving it in, or returning it to the middle of the ground, going himself to Red.

(In dealing with the middle or stepping-stone ball previous to making each of the four corner hoops, both going and returning, there are two distinct methods that may be followed. The Take Off method, or the Stop Shot and Drive method. If Blue has followed the former method he will have roqueted Black gently, and taken off to get his rush on Red for the First Hoop. If he has followed the latter method he will have obtained a rush on Black to somewhere on the boundary behind the First Hoop, and then returned it to the middle of the ground with a Stop Shot or Drive, himself, of course, getting a rush on Red for the First Hoop.

In some cases a player may use whichever method he prefers, but usually one of the methods is clearly indicated by circumstances to the exclusion of the other. And the said circumstances boil down to the all-important Pioneer-Ball-hoop-rush-line. For example, in the present case, if Red were in the neighbourhood of E, the Take Off system would be the better, but if it were—as, in fact, we have placed it—at B, the rush to the boundary behind the First Hoop and the Stop Shot or Drive method would be best.

Please never forget that the all-important factor is always the Pioneer-Ball-hoop-rush-line, from some point in which your Preliminary Approach must be made.

The importance of making the Preliminary Approach from a point in the Pioneer-Ball-hoop-rush-line cannot be overemphasized. It may be said with truth that the difference between a first-class player, who usually " goes round " when he gets his break going, and a medium player, who " goes round " when he is on the top of his game but usually fails

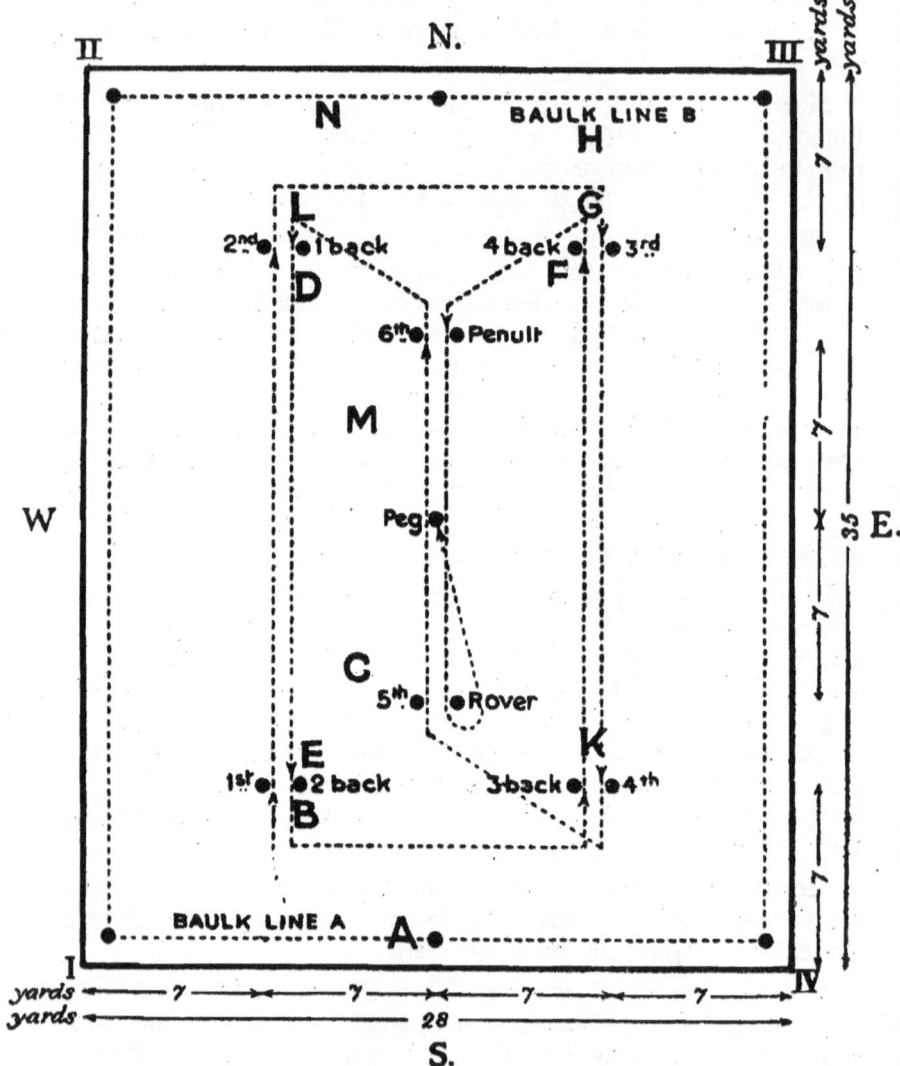

THE FOUR BALL BREAK

otherwise, is just this one thing, that the first-class player has the all-important Rush-line in his mind the whole time, whereas the medium player ignores it. Study the Rush Line Diagrams on Pages 52 and 53.

In those cases where there is complete freedom of choice we, on the whole, prefer the Stop Shot or Drive method to the Take Off system, because we believe that there is a greater margin of error in Stop Shots and Drives than in Take Offs. Also when you use a Stop Shot or Drive your ball runs more steadily than in a Take Off, and is less at the mercy of any possible unevenness in the ground as it slows down.

Though what has been said will have a bearing on the break right on to the end, it will not be continually repeated.

Blue now makes the First Hoop on Red, then croquets Red to F or G near the Third Hoop, going himself to near Black. Blue roquets Black according to the foregoing instructions, then croquets it, leaving it in or returning it to the middle of the ground, and going himself to Yellow.

Blue makes the Second Hoop off Yellow, then croquets Yellow to the Fourth Hoop, preferably to K, going himself to Black. Blue roquets Black, and croquets it, leaving it in or returning it to the middle of the ground, and going himself to Red. (If Red is at G, the Preliminary Approach should be played from H.)

Blue makes the Third Hoop off Red, and then sends Red to the Fifth Hoop, going himself to Black. He roquets and croquets Black, leaving it in or returning it to the middle of the ground, going himself to Yellow.

Blue makes the Fourth Hoop off Yellow, then croquets it to the Sixth Hoop, going himself to near Black. Blue roquets and croquets Black, leaving it in or returning it to the middle of the ground, and going himself to Red.

Blue makes the Fifth Hoop off Red, then croquets Red to near 1 Back, preferably to L, going himself to Black. Blue roquets and croquets Black, leaving it in or returning it to the middle of the ground (but in this case the "middle of the ground" means somewhere near M), and goes himself to Yellow.

THE FOUR BALL BREAK

Blue makes the Sixth Hoop off Yellow, then croquets Yellow to 2 Back, going himself to Black. Blue roquets and croquets Black, leaving it in or returning it to the middle of the ground, and goes himself to Red. (If Red was at L, he should have obtained a rush on Black to N. If Red was at D, he might have correctly rushed Black to M for a Take Off Preliminary Approach, or in the direction of N for a Stop Shot or Drive Preliminary Approach, using the extension of the Rush-line beyond Red.)

From this point Blue's return journey will be similar to the journey out, so at this point we will take leave of him, wishing him luck, and advising him once again not to forget the all-important Rush-line.

But now we must return to the Third Hoop, because at this stage in the break Blue had an alternative that is often to be preferred.

Having made the Third Hoop off Red he might have croqueted Red to the Sixth Hoop, himself getting a rush on Black towards K. He could then have croqueted Black to the Fifth Hoop, going himself to Yellow. To do this he would probably have had to use a Split Drive or Split Roll. But as it would have been only a short and easy stroke this would not have mattered.

(If Blue were following this method he should take special care of his rush towards Yellow. He must not only bear in mind the Yellow-fourth-hoop-rush-line, but he must beware of rushing Black so close to Yellow that he has not room to send it to the Fifth Hoop.)

Blue then makes the Fourth Hoop off Yellow, then sends it to the middle of the ground, going himself to Black. He makes the Fifth Hoop off Black, then croquets Black to 1 Back, going himself to Yellow. Except for the colour of the balls, his progress will now be the same as before, so we will leave him to carry on.

(In proceeding from the Fifth Hoop to 1 Back there is a variety of methods that may be used, according to the pleasure of the player, and provided he keeps in his mind the all-important Rush-lines, he can safely exercise a wide choice.

THE FOUR BALL BREAK

By the by—and this is most important—the "middle of the ground" as applied to the middle or stepping-stone ball is an elastic term. The Middle Ball is not a fixture to the freehold but a movable object. And one of its special uses is to enable the player to repair the damage done to his break by a bad stroke. If, for example, a Pioneer Ball for one of the outside hoops has been sent too far, the Middle Ball can still be rushed on to the Rush-line behind it, and the situation thus saved.

It is well to remember that a Four Ball Break that has begun to go wrong, can often be repaired by sending two balls close to one another, so that after roqueting one, a rush can be obtained on the other to the next hoop. If you are for Three Back, for example, you are in a much stronger position if you have two balls together not from the Fifth Hoop, than if you had your Pioneer Ball for Three Back badly placed, and your Middle Ball a long way away.

X

THE THREE BALL BREAK

In theory the Three Ball Break is easier than the Four Ball Break, since there are only two assistant balls, which are used alternatively for making the points; in fact, however, it is considerably more difficult, since there is no convenient middle or stepping-stone ball for helping things along, and for facilitating a recovery after a bad stroke!

We will start, as before, with Blue and Yellow at A, and Red at B. Diagram on next page.

Blue roquets Yellow, then croquets it to D at the Second Hoop, going himself to Red. He makes the First Hoop off Red, then sends Red to K or H at the Third Hoop, going himself to near Yellow.

(In croqueting Yellow to D, Blue had to use a Stop Shot and take great care to get on to the Red-first-hoop-rush-line. In making the First Hoop he had to try and get a rush up the ground, to a convenient spot for Splitting Red to K or H and himself getting on to the Yellow-second-hoop-rush-line.

Now in the Three Ball Break it will not always be possible to play the Preliminary Approach from a spot in the Pioneer-Ball-hoop-rush-line; in all such cases please bear in mind that it is urgently necessary to play for, and use, a Double Stroke with a large margin of error. Stop Shots, Drives, Sharp Splits and Split Drives have a much larger margin of error than Take-Offs.

In Blue's progress to Yellow at the Second Hoop, if Yellow is at D, Red should if possible be rushed to E. Should this not be possible it would be all right to rush Red to F, which would give an easy Stop Shot for putting it across to the Third Hoop.

Should Yellow have gone too far, and be in the neighbourhood of G, Red should if possible be rushed into the Second Corner; which would give an easy Stop Shot, with a little " split " in it putting Red across to the Third Hoop.

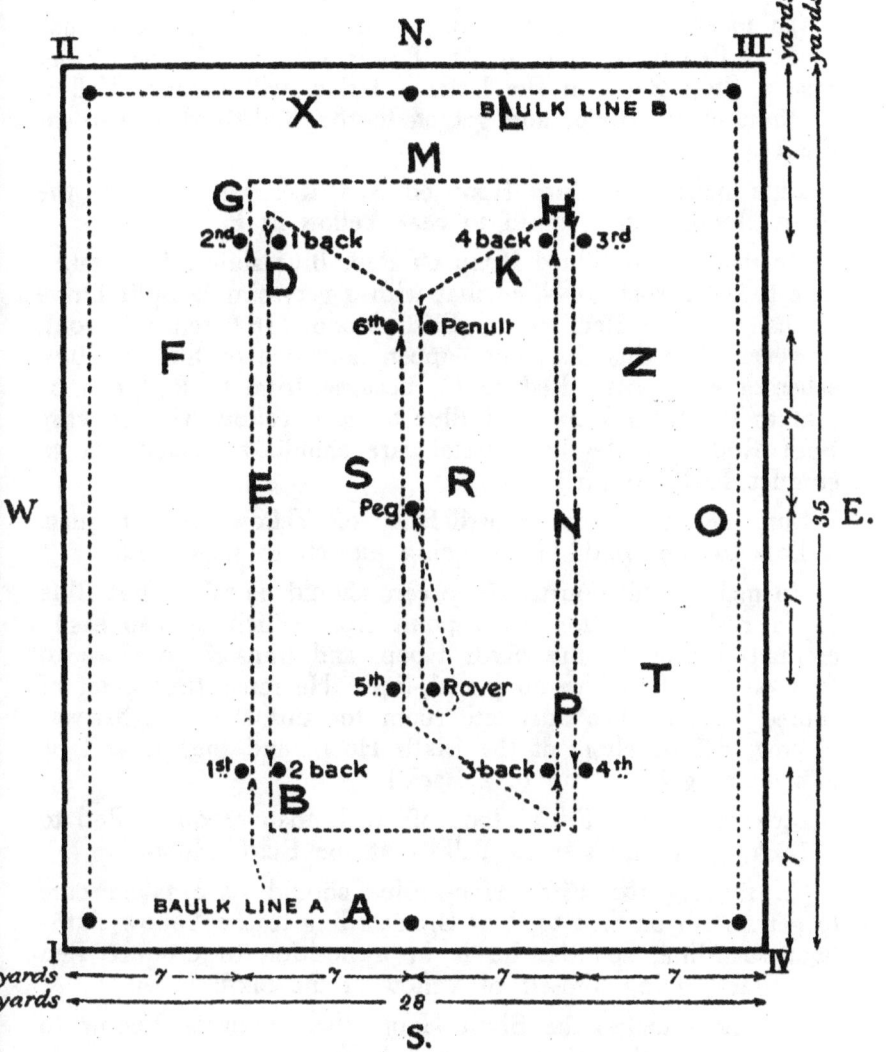

THE THREE BALL BREAK

Blue makes the Second Hoop off Yellow, then sends Yellow to the Fourth Hoop, going himself to Red at the Third Hoop.

(In making the Second Hoop Blue should have got a rush to L, if Red is at H; or to M, if Red is at K. In the former case a Stop Shot, in the latter a Drive, will croquet Yellow to the Fourth Hoop, and get on to the Red-third-hoop-rush-line.)

Blue makes the Third Hoop off Red, then sends Red to the Fifth Hoop, going himself to near Yellow at P.

(In making the Third Hoop off Red, Blue should have taken care to get a rush to N, so that with a very simple Split Drive he can croquet Red to the Fifth Hoop. It often falls out, however, that this does not happen, and one of the next best schemes is to rush Red to O, because from O Red can be sent to the Fifth Hoop and Blue to near Yellow with an easy Split Roll. By the by, special care should be taken not to croquet Red too far.)

Blue now makes the Fourth Hoop off Yellow, then croquets Yellow to the Sixth Hoop, going himself to near Red.

(In making the Fourth Hoop care should be taken that Blue has a rush on Yellow to a point from which he can easily croquet Yellow to the Sixth Hoop, and himself go close to Red on the Red-fifth-hoop-rush-line. He must take care, of course, that he has adequate room for this stroke, otherwise Yellow will be short of the Sixth Hoop, and then it will be difficult to get Red up to 1 Back.)

Blue makes the Fifth Hoop off Red, then croquets Red to 1 Back, going himself to Yellow at the Sixth Hoop.

(In making the Fifth Hoop Blue should have taken care to get a rush on Red to R or S, according to the Yellow-sixth-hoop-rush-line, so that he is in a position to croquet Red to 1 Back, going himself to Yellow at the Sixth Hoop.)

Blue now makes the Sixth Hoop, then croquets Yellow to 2 Back, going himself to Red at 1 Back.

(Blue should have taken very great care in making the Sixth Hoop, to get a rush to X, so that he can easily croquet Yellow to 2 Back, himself getting a rush on Red for 1 Back.)

THE THREE BALL BREAK

From this point his progress will be similar to that of the outward journey, and so we will now take leave of him.

Now the Three Ball Break, as we have outlined it, is the Three Ball Break as it *should* be played. But it does not by any means always happen that way even with first-class players. In making hoops, rushes are often overrun, so that the player, having run the First Hoop, for example, may find himself under the necessity of sending Red—we keep the colours as before for convenience sake—sending Red to the Third Hoop and going himself to near Yellow at the Second Hoop with a difficult long Split Roll. And at the Second Hoop he may have to croquet Yellow to the Fourth Hoop with a difficult Split Drive, going himself to Red at the Third Hoop. And, most difficult of all, when he has made the Third Hoop off Red he may find himself under the necessity of croqueting Red to the Fifth Hoop and going himself to Yellow at the Fourth Hoop with a slightly split Pass Roll. He should, therefore, in his practise not only try to play the Three Ball Break the easiest way but make himself familiar with these heavy, difficult strokes. For his encouragement it may be said that though these strokes are unquestionably difficult they can be mastered with practice!

In an actual game Blue would probably not proceed far with his Three Ball Break without arranging to bring in Black, and turn it into a Four Ball Break. For example, if Black were in the Second Corner, Blue in making the First Hoop would take care to get a rush to the neighbourhood of F. From this point with a thick Take Off he would leave Red in the middle of the ground and go himself to near Black. He would then roquet Black and croquet it to the Third Hoop, going himself to Yellow at the Second Hoop. He would then have a Four Ball Break.

If Black were in the Third Corner, on making the Second Hoop Blue would rush Yellow to the neighbourhood of Z, Take Off to Black, then croquet Black to the Fourth Hoop, going himself to Red at the Third Hoop.

If Black were in the Fourth Corner, Blue, in making the Third Hoop off Red, would get a rush to T. Take Off to

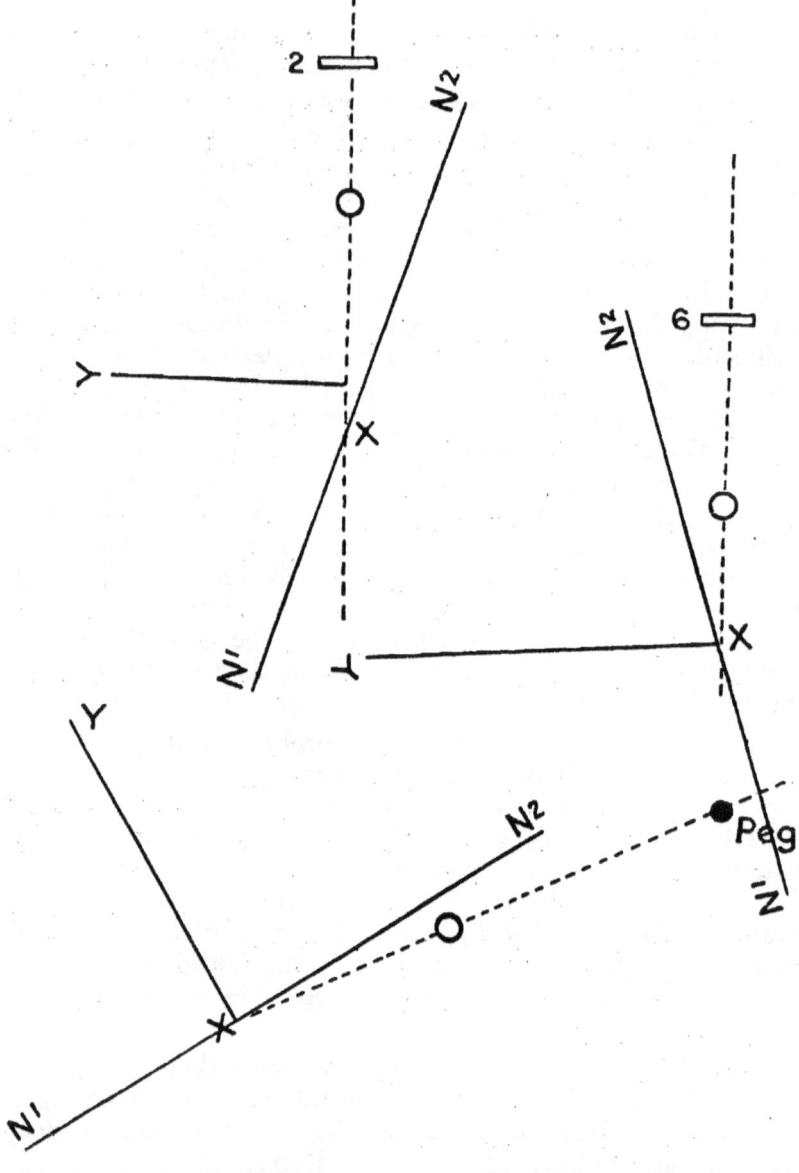

A point in the Rush Line—at or near X—is the ideal place from which to play the Preliminary Approach; but any point between N1 and X, or even between N2 and X, is greatly to be preferred from running across the Rush Line from Y.

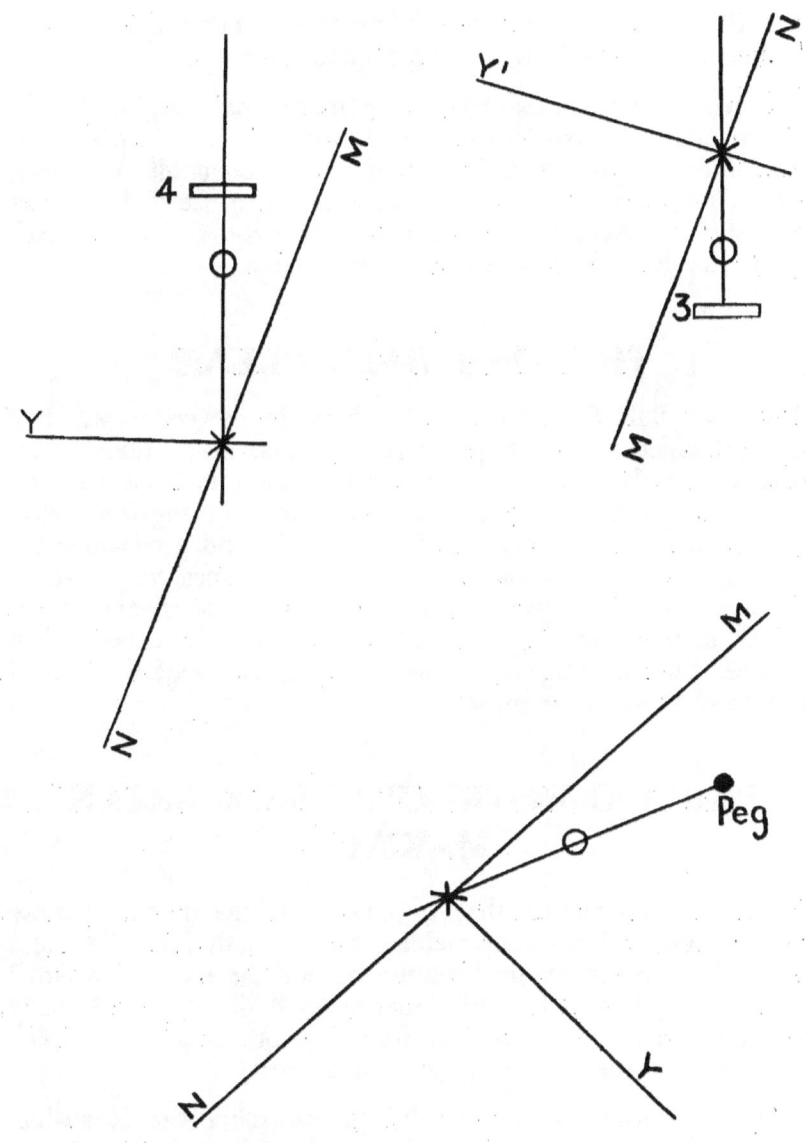

A point in the Rush Line—at or near X—is the ideal place from which to play the Preliminary Approach; but a point between N and X, or even between M and X, is much to be preferred from running across the Rush Line from Y.

near Black and then croquet Black to the Fifth Hoop, going himself to near Yellow at the Fourth Hoop.

It need hardly be said that the matter of bringing in the Fourth Ball is usually so important that it justifies the Preliminary Approach being played from a point off the Rush-line. Care, however, must always be taken to use those strokes that have the greatest possible margin of error, and to get back on to the Rush-line as quickly as possible.

THE TWO BALL BREAK

THE Two Ball Break, *i.e.*, a break made by your own ball and one assistant ball, requires few detailed instructions. Its success depends on accurate Approaches, accurate Hoop-running so as to obtain rushes, and accurate rushing; together with, quite frankly, an occasional desperate stroke and a considerable slice of luck! It is good fun, and sometimes very useful. For example, it is quite often the best way of getting from 4 Back to the Winning Peg, and getting out. It is well worth practice, but no player, however expert, can regard it as a reliable method of progress.

PARTING INSTRUCTIONS ON BREAK MAKING

IT will be appreciated that to deal with the infinite variety of situations that arise in making breaks, both Four Ball and Three Ball Breaks, would be quite beyond the scope of a small Handbook. It would require many pages of print and many more diagrams. We must therefore close our Section on Break Making with the following general advice:—

(1) You cannot be too careful to remember the Rush-line system. Playing Preliminary Approaches from points in or near the Rush Line, or even near the extension of the Rush Line is an essential of successful break-making. Running across the Rush Line at right angles is the road to failure.

PARTING INSTRUCTIONS ON BREAK MAKING

(2) In dealing with the Middle Ball in the Four Ball Break, remember that the term Middle Ball is an elastic one, and that your method of dealing with it must always be governed by the position of the next Hoop Rush-line. It will, in fact, very often have to be driven and left temporarily very far from the middle of the ground.

(3) Remember to choose the strokes, as far as possible, that have the greatest margin of error.

(4) In croqueting the Pioneer Ball to the next Hoop-but-one, send it well up to the Hoop; but it is better to have it considerably short rather than slightly too far.

(5) IF YOUR NEXT STROKE IS AN EASY ONE, DON'T TREAT IT WITH CONTEMPT! INSTEAD, TREAT IT AS A PRICELESS OPPORTUNITY TO IMPROVE THE GENERAL POSITION. Experts and "likely players" are scrupulously careful over easy strokes. Persons - who - never - will - improve treat easy strokes with contempt.

(6) Croquet balls have no special inclination to run naturally to "book positions"; therefore, when things do not happen according to plan do not be disconcerted or discouraged; instead, bring to your aid such of the standard strokes of the game as you have mastered by practice, and the knowledge of the principles underlying break making—which have been clearly set forth in the foregoing pages—to carry on, and restore the position.

HOW TO PICK UP BREAKS

To become expert in picking up breaks you need four things: *common-sense, imagination, a thorough knowledge of the Rush-line Theory, and a thorough knowledge of what can be done by the ordinary standard strokes of the game.*

Given these ingredients, here are a few examples of what can be done: —

(1) This example is purely elementary, nevertheless it illustrates what might be described as probably the most usual method of picking up a break. The method is as follows: — Having roqueted Assistant Ball One, this is croqueted to the next-hoop-but-one as Pioneer Ball, at the same time a rush is obtained on Assistant Ball Two to the Third-assistant-ball-and-next-hoop-rush-line. Please get this method well into mind, because it may with truth be described as the basic method of picking up breaks.

Here is our particular example. Blue is for the First Hoop. Yellow has broken down on Blue at the Fifth Hoop. Black is in the middle of the ground. Red is just in front of the Sixth Hoop. Blue roquets Yellow. With a Split Drive he sends Yellow to the Second Hoop, taking care himself to get a rush on Black towards the Red-first-hoop-rush-line. Having duly rushed Black, he roquets it, leaving it in the middle of the ground and himself getting his rush on Red for the First Hoop. He rushes Red to the First Hoop, and is in possession of a Four Ball Break.

(2) Blue has roqueted Black on the boundary behind the First Hoop, which is Blue's Hoop. Red is somewhere between the First and Second Hoops. Yellow is a long way away not available for any help. Blue is inclined to give up any attempt to get on that turn. It would obviously be a very difficult stroke to roll Black to the Second Hoop and get a rush back on Red to the First. But, just one moment, Blue remembers one of the standard strokes. A Stop Shot would put Black up to the Second Hoop and Blue in position for the First. He could then run it with a free stroke right down to Red. He would then be possessed of a Three Ball Break.

HOW TO PICK UP BREAKS

(3) Now suppose Red, instead of being somewhere between the First and Second Hoops, had been with Yellow in the Second Corner. Blue could still pick up the break in similar fashion. Using a Drive instead of a Stop Shot he could approach the First Hoop, and then run it so as to get a rush up the ground to Black; then with a Split Roll he could send Black to the Third Hoop, going himself to the enemy's balls in the Second Corner. He could then roquet one, and get a rush on the other to the Second Hoop. Having made the Second Hoop he could take off to the ball left near the corner, roquet it, and then with a long Split Roll croquet it to the Fourth Hoop, going himself to Black at the Third. This example is advanced Croquet, nevertheless it is the kind of thing that an enterprising player must have in his mind. It is the kind of thing, too, that wins games!

(4) Take another position. Blue is in the Third Corner, Black two feet away on the shorter boundary. Red and Yellow are in the First Corner. Blue is for the Second Hoop. Probably Blue's first thought is about getting to Red and Yellow. Then it occurs to him that, with luck, he might perhaps cut Black up to the Second Hoop. But, wait a minute! He can do something much better than that! He should cut Black as near the Third Hoop as he safely can. He then takes off to Red and Yellow. Roquets one, and gets a rush on the other towards his Second Hoop. He rushes Red or Yellow to the Second Hoop, and he has achieved a Three Ball Break.

(5) Again, Yellow, playing a Three Ball Break, has broken down on Blue at the Third Hoop. Black is in the First Corner. Blue is for the First Hoop. Red is near the Fourth Hoop. Black is for the Second Hoop. Blue roquets Yellow, then wonders what to do. To start with he finds that the Third Hoop is too much in his way for him to try and split Yellow to the Second Hoop and get a rush on Red to his First Hoop. In any case, perhaps he would have been rightly afraid of this really difficult stroke. But he has quite a good game that he can play on the safe side. Blue Takes Off to Red, leaving Yellow near the Third Hoop. Then with a Split Roll, he croquets Red to the Second Hoop, going himself to

Black. He then tries a roll approach to the First Hoop. If he succeeds, he has gained a Four Ball Break. If he fails he can leave a well-laid Break for Black.

We could add many more examples; but we think that we have given enough to show how breaks can be picked up; with the use of the ingredients already mentioned!

By the bye, the examples given are examples of what can be done, but not rigid rules to be obeyed slavishly in every case when the position indicated, or one like it, happens to have developed. In a particular match, the capacity of the Player, the strength of the opponent, the state of the game, and the quality of the ground, whether fast or slow, are all factors to be carefully considered.

One more piece of advice on picking up breaks: over-adventurousness and enterprise may occasionally lose you a game, that greater caution would have won. But over-caution and lack of enterprise will effectively prevent you from progress towards becoming a first-class player.

XII

HOW TO LAY BREAKS

IN modern Croquet there are three methods of laying the Break. They may be described as the Cross Wire or Cross Peg method; the partial Wire method; and the Open method. To start with we will explain each of these methods with reference to the First Hoop.

(1) Red and Yellow are left Cross Wired at the First Hoop, that is, of course, one on each side of the Hoop say at A and B wired from each other. Black is taken to the Third Corner, say at C, and left with a comfortable rush on Blue to the First Hoop. Before the coming of the present Law 44, this was the usual method of ending a first break in A Opens.

(2) Red is near the Second Hoop at E, Yellow is just beyond the First Hoop at D, carefully wired from Blue and Black at F. Black has a rush on Blue for the First Hoop.

(3) Red is near the First Hoop, shall we say at B. Yellow is near the Second Hoop at E. Blue and Black are at G. Black has a rush on the First Hoop, but this rush has been laid with sufficient care not to give either Red or Yellow a double shot.

The order of merit of these three methods is as we have given them. Obviously Method 1 is the best, because it gives the adversary the longest possible shot, and the player an easy get-away. Method 2 is better than 3, because the get-away if the shot of the adversary has been missed, is easier.

In an actual game however, it is usually necessary to be in full possession of the balls with a Four Ball Break to be able to use either Method 1 or Method 2, whereas Method 3 can be brought into use in very many cases.

Here is some advice as to how to bring Methods 1 and 2 into use, when you have established full control with a Four Ball Break. Suppose Blue desires to leave off his Break after making Three Back, leaving Red and Yellow cross-wired at the First Hoop, ready for Black. Blue must take care to arrange his break, so that he makes Two back off an enemy ball. He must also bring up Black close at hand, so that when he has run the hoop, and carefully wired Red and Yellow on

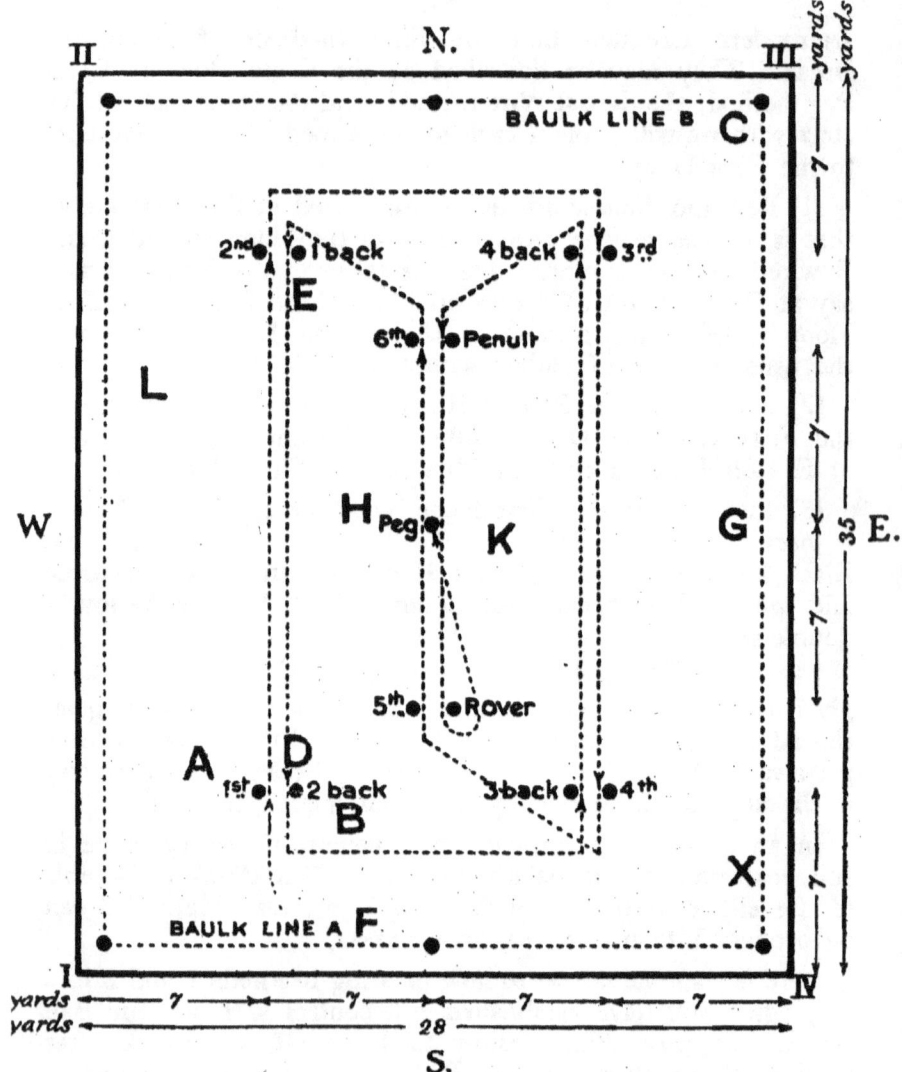

HOW TO LAY BREAKS

each side of it, he can rush his Black down to Three Back, make Three Black off Black, and then, according to circumstances, take it away to a safe distance, leaving Black a good rush towards the First Hoop.

We will now give in greater detail a First Class Player's method of achieving the cross-wire at the Peg at the end of his first break. He will try as soon as possible to make the partner-ball the middle ball. This is important. We will therefore suppose that he has successfully arranged for his partner-ball to be the middle ball in his progress up the centre of the Court through the Fifth and Sixth Hoops. If so the position may be as follows: The Player Blue is about to make One Back off Red. Black is in the middle of the ground. Yellow is at Two Back.

Blue makes One Back off Red, then croquets Red to Three Back, going himself to Black. He roquets and croquets Black, leaving it in, or returning it to the middle of the ground near the Peg, and going himself to Yellow. He makes Two Back off Yellow, taking care to get a rush on Yellow to the middle of the ground near Black. He rushes Yellow near to the Peg, then very carefully taking-off from it, he goes to Black; he roquets and croquets Black, taking-off from it to Red; and using great care to leave Black and Yellow on the same side of the Peg, near together. Blue makes Three Back off Red, taking great care to get a rush on Red to a point just beyond Yellow. Blue then rushes Red, then croquets Red to the other side of the Peg, with a small Stop Shot, taking the utmost possible care to get a rush on Yellow to a spot dead-pegged from Red. Blue then rushes Yellow to the pegged spot, then croquets it with the utmost possible care, so as to leave it pegged, and gets a rush on Black to the Fourth Corner. He rushes Black towards the Fourth Corner, say to X, then takes the utmost care to lay Blue and Black, so that Black has a rush towards the Peg, but that there is no double-target for either Red or Yellow on each side of the Peg, say at H and K, nor from either Baulk. Obviously this is something that altogether, as should be the case, will require first class play from a first class player.

There are two important things to remember for Cross-Pegs and Cross-wires. You must never make the last Hoop of your Break off your Partner Ball; and, when you are doing the Cross-pegging or cross-wiring, try to do it all from one side of the Peg or Hoop. The attempt to tidy up on both sides is a very frequent cause of failure. By the bye, should it become obvious that a Cross-Peg is unlikely to be successful, another method that can be, and, in fact, is often adopted, is to dismiss one ball to L, about three yards from the boundary, leaving the other one at K, and taking your own and partner ball to X as before. If the opponent misses and you have a rush on partner ball to L, which is important, you still have good prospects of progress, in spite of your having failed to achieve a Cross Peg. After the name of a famous player, this leave is called the Whichelo Leave.

Method 2 usually comes in as a makeshift, in cases where a Cross-wire at the First Hoop would have been expedient, but has not been achieved. We will suppose that Blue has run One Back, that the other three balls are at hand; but that Blue finds it is too risky to try for the Cross-wire. He has rushed Yellow or Red too far, or what not. In such a case, he might dismiss Red or Yellow to the Second Hoop, and leave the other the wrong side of the First Hoop, getting a rush on Black to some point in Baulk A carefully wired from the enemy just beyond the First Hoop. This scheme has the merit that, if the enemy misses, the partner ball has a very easy get-away.

Method 3 is the method for occasions when no break has given any control. One enemy ball is dismissed to the next-hoop-but-one, the other to the next Hoop, one's own ball (player or partner) is left with a good rush on the next Hoop.

We would conclude this Chapter on Break Laying by remarking that one of the things that makes Croquet so interesting and fascinating is the necessity of meeting all sorts of different, and indeed endlessly varying situations, with thoughtfulness and resource.

XIII

THE OPENINGS

WE shall content ourselves with the conventional openings, and leave what may be described as experimental openings to those experts who have an inclination to experiment.

Assuming that tossing formalities are over, and that Blue and Black on the one side, and Red and Yellow on the other, are ready for the fray, and that Blue and Black have won the toss and are starting (the opponent having chosen Red and Yellow) Blue will lead off by going to A, a foot or so from the Fourth Corner on the long boundary. Red will reply by laying a Tice and going to B. The length of this Tice is a matter for consideration. It must be long enough to be missable by Black, but it should not be so long that there is little chance of Yellow hitting it.

Black now has a choice! Shall he go to D, a couple of feet from Blue on the long boundary, or shall he shoot at Red? He will ask himself two questions. What is the chance of my hitting it? If I go to D, what is the chance of Yellow hitting it? If he comes to the conclusion that it is a long Tice and that Yellow may easily miss it, he will go to D. If he feels that Yellow would be pretty sure to hit it, he will shoot at Red.

If Black hits Red he should croquet it to D, not minding whether it goes off or not, going himself to the neighbourhood of E. Yellow, of course, must govern his actions on what Black has done. If Black is at E, and Blue and Red at A and D, Yellow had better take a shot at Black, so that if he misses, he will go well out of the game somewhere near the Third Corner. If he should hit, he would, of course, Take Off to Blue and Red, roquet one—preferably Blue—and get a rush on the other to his First Hoop. Should he be successful he might make the First Hoop off, shall we say, Red, then send Red to the Third Hoop getting a rush on Black to the Second Hoop. He will then have a Three Ball Break, which he can convert into a Four Ball Break at the Fourth Hoop.

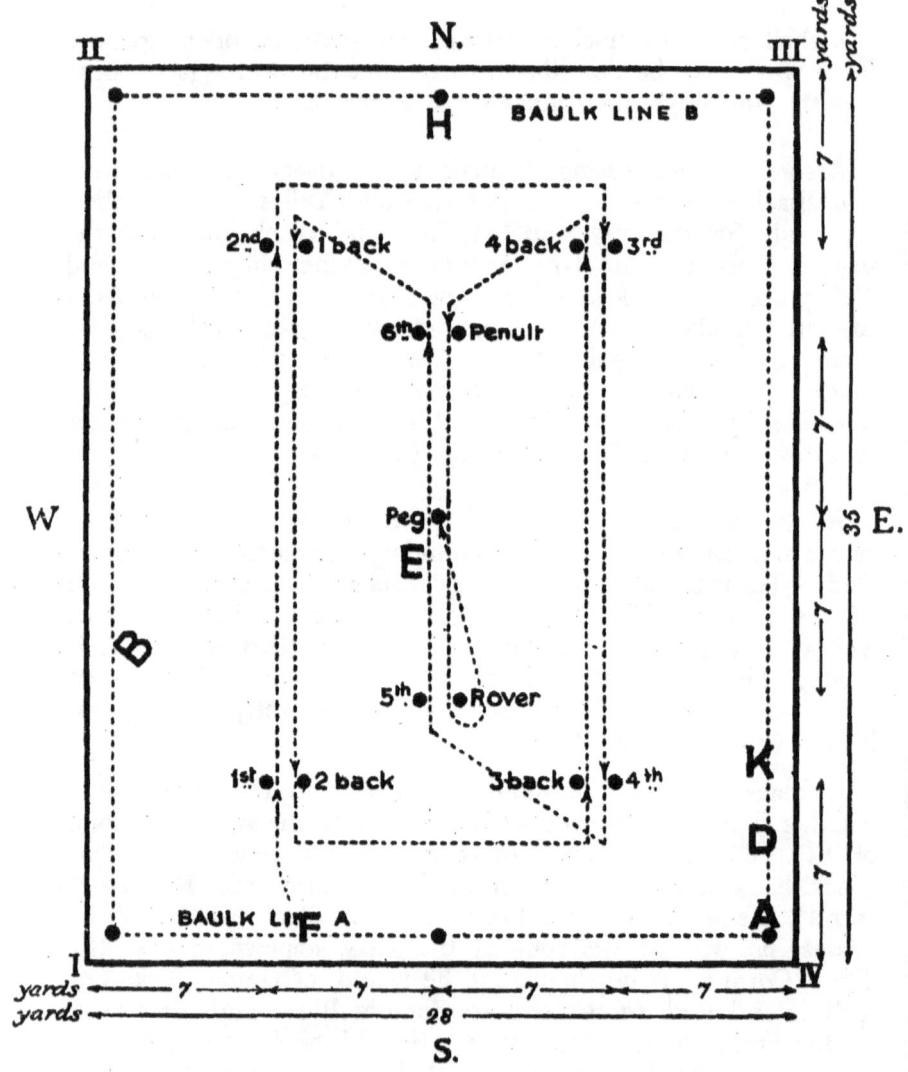

THE OPENINGS

We must retrace our steps! Suppose Black missed Red, running down towards the Second Corner. In this case Yellow must shoot at Red from F, so as to be sure to remain near it. Should he hit, he can roll his balls towards the First Corner, leaving a rush on the First Hoop. Should he miss, Black may reply by shooting back at Red and Yellow. If he should hit, he might obtain a chance of a break, failing which he can lay the break for Blue on the Open System. If Black should miss, Yellow can rush Red to Black, get another rush and make the First Hoop. He might with luck get a rush back to Red and snatch the Second Hoop, but it is more than likely that he will have to be satisfied with dismissing Black, laying Red a rush on the First Hoop and awaiting a more favourable moment for getting away.

If, on the other hand, Black did not shoot at Red, but instead went to D, Yellow must shoot at Red from the First Corner. If he does this successfully he may rush Red towards the Second Hoop, in which case, by taking off to Blue and Black near the Fourth Corner, he may obtain a Three Ball Break.

Should Yellow miss Red, Blue should rush Black to K, and lay himself a rush on Black to the First Hoop.

At this point Red will probably reply by going to H, at least five yards from where Yellow is reposing.

Blue will now rush Black to the First Hoop, make the First Hoop off Black, and then one way or another go down and separate Red and Yellow. With skill and luck—he would need both—he might even collect a break.

At this juncture we may say that the Opening stage of the game is concluded, and that the battle has been fully joined. We must therefore leave Blue and Black and Red and Yellow to fight it out, each side using his or her knowledge of the standard strokes of the game, and of the methods of picking up, and making breaks to give a good account of himself or herself in the fray.

XIV

TACTICS OF THE OUT-PLAYER

THE man or woman or partners sitting over there watching the progress of the In-player or Players are Out-players. The Out-player has one big question in his mind, how and when will he get in? He knows, of course, that there are just two ways in which he may get in, through the adversary breaking down, or through a good long shot of his own. He or she therefore looks both with interest and hope at everything that the In-player does. But if the In-player completes his turn without a breakdown, the Out-player is faced with these questions:—Shall I shoot, or must I play my ball to some place on the boundary, where the adversary will not be able to make effective use of it? If I decide to shoot, which ball shall I shoot at? These momentous questions can only be answered by finding answers to two further questions. If I shoot at this or that ball, what shall I be able to get out of it? If I miss, what shall I give away?

It is quite possible to have your mind so centred on what you might be able to do as a result of a successful shot, that you entirely overlook the consequences of a miss. It is equally possible to be so obsessed with the fear of the results of a miss that you overlook the tremendous prize that a hit would put within your grasp.

Here are a few suggestions for solving this problem. If you are playing against a player very much better than yourself, it is often wise to err on the side of adventure rather than on the side of caution. The reason is this, that if you pick off a shot when the balls are well placed for your progress you may make a good break, whereas if you yield to caution your very superior opponent may still be able to use your ball, and the only result of your caution will be that you have lost a chance. It is not always easy for an inferior player to determine how a very much better player may be able to turn ball positions to his use.

On the other hand, if you are playing against a player about equal to yourself it will be a great mistake to present him with opportunities, which he would not be able to gain for himself, by too much shooting into his game.

Other things being equal, you will naturally choose to shoot at, if you decide to shoot, the ball that will give you the best chance of getting on. In order to determine this, you will have to go back to your old friend the rush-line, and say to yourself: "If I shoot and hit, shall we say Red, I shall be able to send Red to my next Hoop but one, and at the same time get a rush on Yellow to my Black-first-hoop-rush-line." This is the formula again and again.

It often happens, however, that it is best to shoot, but desirable to shoot at a ball which will not give immediate prospects of a Break. This happens, of course, when you can combine shooting with playing for safety. Obviously, it is better to shoot with the possibility of at least gaining the innings than merely to play a waiting game by going on to a boundary, that is, of course, when this can be done with equal safety.

One more piece of advice for the Out-player. Towards the end of a game it very often pays to join close or fairly close on a distant boundary. Suppose, for example, Yellow is for the Peg, and Red has some sort of a rush on Yellow for the Penultimate. Suppose Black is near the First Corner, and Blue somewhere in the neighbourhood of the Second Corner. In this case, if shooting at Red and Yellow would mean that Blue or Black, whichever took the shot, if it should miss would land on a distant boundary remote from everyone, it would be better unless Red were a super-crack for Blue to join Black. It would be much less comfortable for Red to rush Yellow to the Penultimate, and perhaps have to make a long Approach, if, so to speak, he was looking over his shoulder at Red and Yellow adjacent to one another, and both ready and willing to pounce on him, if anything went wrong. Whereas, if after your shot Blue and Black were still widely separated, Red could go ahead with his rush and approach with the comfortable feeling that even a mishap would not necessarily deprive him of the innings.

XV

THE END OF THE GAME

WITH regard to the end of the game, we do not propose to give detailed instructions, but rather to give some general advice, especially to beginners and very medium players.

When you began your game—assuming, of course, that it was something more than the merest knock-up—you felt that before the end you had a long way to go, and so probably you were not particularly nervous or excited, but when you see partner ball's clip on the Peg, and you have only Last Hoop, or the last two or three hoops to make, it is a very different state of things. You will be feeling not a little excited, and possibly more than a little nervous. Therefore, if you are IN and making the last hoops take the utmost possible care to make things easy for yourself. However small the strokes that you have to make, however easy they seem, yet take the last ounce of care of your rush-lines and hoop approaches. It will make all the difference to you if you find yourself by careful play just one foot from the last hoop right in front. The Rover Hoop seems to greet us with a derisive smile if we find that we are too far away and a bit at the side!

As to laying the break for going out, though it is true that a first-class player playing a first-class player would seldom leave balls in the middle of the ground, it may often pay the beginner or medium player to take one risk of the enemy hitting in order to make as sure as possible of getting out next time. After all, you will gain nothing by laying your break so difficult for yourself that you break down and leave the balls in the middle of the ground that way.

One final word. Do not imagine that the game is over when you give a sigh of relief because you are through the last Hoop, and have every reason to expect that you are about to peg out both balls. Do not relax your care by a hair's breadth until *both* balls have been pegged out. There is no such thing as a shot so easy that it never has been, and could not be, missed!

And, when you are *lining up your balls* for the peg out, do not hurry. Look at your line up near, and look at it far, and look at it also from the other side of the Peg. Do not be too excited or nervous to take your time.

THE END OF THE GAME

In connection with the end of the game, if you should gain the innings, when your opponent has one ball a Rover, and have the opportunity of doing so, there is the question whether you should or should not peg him out. In order to answer this question, you must clearly understand what are the advantages to be gained by pegging out an adversary, and what the disadvantages are. The advantage of pegging out an opponent is that you entirely deprive him of all power of combination. He cannot gain and retain the innings. The disadvantage is that you lose the fourth ball, and thereby retard your own progress. Playing an inferior player, likely to be disconcerted by being pegged out, you should not hesitate for a moment. Playing someone of your own strength, you should not hesitate if you have only a few points to make with your non-Rover ball, and he has many. And sometimes, even if you have more points to make than the adversary—especially if he does not happen to be a super-shot—it will pay you to peg him out. With one possible exception, never peg out one of two Rovers. The one exception is this: If in a double one Rover is a super-shot and the other a very poor shot, it would probably be worth while to peg out the super-shot; assuming, of course, you have only a few points to make.

When you have pegged out an adversary you must take all possible care to give yourself comfortable rushes to your hoop well out of his way, and wired from him whenever possible. Be very careful never to give him a double target. Sometimes, if you have established a substantial lead, it pays to peg out your own Rover and finish the match as a two-ball game.

XVI

THE TRIPLE AND DOUBLE PEELS

THE Triple and Double Peels definitely belong to advanced Croquet and therefore they do not properly come within the scope of this little Book, nevertheless, a modern book on Croquet would hardly be complete which ignored the Peels. Therefore we include the following brief notes on "how the trick is done."

The Triple and Double Peels, and we put them together as the former includes the latter, amount to the Four Ball Break with a decoration!

When opportunity offers, a first-class player who has one Clip on 4 Back and is beginning his second all-round break will endeavour to peel the partner-ball through the last three hoops, and run out in the one turn.

His method will be to use the partner-ball for making the Third Hoop, having taken care to bring the middle-ball also near the hoop. In approaching the hoop he will croquet the partner-ball just in front of the 4 Back side. He will run the Third Hoop himself, then peel the partner-ball through the 4 Back, taking care to get a rush himself on the middle ball in the direction of the Fourth Hoop, so that he can easily get on to the Pioneer-ball-fourth-hoop-rush-line.

When he comes to make the Fourth Hoop he will use every endeavour to get a rush back into the Third Corner. He will then rush the assistant ball to the Third Corner, croquet it back to the neighbourhood of the Sixth Hoop, at the same time getting a rush on the peeled-ball towards the Sixth Hoop. He will rush the peeled-ball to the Sixth Hoop, and then take off to the Pioneer Ball at the Fifth Hoop. At the Sixth Hoop he will use the same method he adopted at the Third. He will have the middle ball quite close, put the partner-ball just in front of the Penultimate. Having run the Sixth Hoop he will peel the partner through the Penultimate, taking care to get a rush on the middle ball to a point from which he can conveniently croquet it to 2 Back, while going himself to his Pioneer Ball at 1 Back.

If possible in his progress either to 2 Back or 3 Back he

TRIPLE AND DOUBLE PEELS

will get a rush on the partner-ball to a spot in front of the last Hoop, and as he goes to his Pioneer Ball at one or the other he will peel the partner through the last Hoop. This is, of course, the best method. But if it cannot be followed he will have to leave the last peel to the end, and do his utmost to be sure of having the partner-ball right in front of the Last Hoop for the all-important Peel. To make things easy, if the Peel comes off, he will have both the other balls at hand, so that, when he has run the Last Hoop himself he can be sure by using first one and then the other of getting on to the all-important Partner-ball-peg-rush-line.

By the by, should the peeled ball be stymied from the Peg by the Last Hoop, it is often possible in taking croquet from one of the other balls to cannon it clear before getting the rush to the Peg.

The difficulty of the Triple and Double Peels does not consist in any particular super-stroke that has to be made, but rather in the fact that a very high level of stroke play has to be maintained from start to finish.

In leaving the subject of the Peels, we would remark that though in a Knock-up Game it is sometimes good fun to start a Triple or Double Peel, even if the ball positions are difficult, and to continue to fight it out so long as there is the slightest chance of bringing it off. This is seldom or never wise in a really important game that you strongly desire to win. In this case by all means try the peels if things shape that way, but the moment things begin to go wrong give up all thought of Peels; try and restore your ball positions, and carry on with the ordinary break.

XVII

MISCELLANEOUS TACTICAL ADVICE

WE have already dealt with various methods of Break-laying. In applying those methods to actual play in a game it must be kept in mind that you have not only to make sure of your own progress, if the adversary obligingly misses his shot, but you have also to take care so to place the balls that he is obliged to shoot at least advantage to himself.

Suppose, for example, that your balls Blue and Black are for the First Hoop, and that Red is for the First Hoop and Yellow for the Second Hoop; we will suppose further that you have just hit a long shot, and that you have not full control, and that your only way of laying a break is the open method, *i.e.*, to send one adversary ball to the Second Hoop, and one to the First Hoop, and leave Blue and Black with a rush a long way away. In such circumstances, and they are circumstances that occur again and again, you must take care to send Yellow to the Second Hoop and Red to the First Hoop; and you must be very careful in placing Blue and Black in the first place not to give a double target (it is a good idea to wire one or other of them, or both if possible, from the nearest of the enemy balls) and, secondly, to be sure that if the enemy shoots at your balls, and misses, he will go where you can make use of him. He is almost sure, as a matter of fact, to shoot with Red, because he will not like to leave it conveniently placed for you at your First Hoop, therefore you must guard Blue and Black from Red's shot, with special care.

Take note of the fact that by placing Red at Red's Hoop, and Yellow at Yellow's Hoop, you are ensuring that whichever shoots is going away from its Hoop, and will have no ball at its Hoop waiting for it, if it should hit.

Through making it difficult for the adversary to get away at once on a break, if he should hit, you are doing two things: you are buying a chance of immediately having your innings restored, if he should try to knock up a difficult break and fail; and you are buying a chance of time yourself to regain the innings by a shot.

MISCELLANEOUS TACTICAL ADVICE

It must, however, be added that in this matter of making things difficult for the adversary should he hit in, much regard must be paid to one's own capabilities. It is no use thinking so much of what the adversary might do that you leave things too difficult for yourself. Also Croquet is a psychological game, and regard has to be paid to one's own state of mind and nerves at the moment. The fact that a player would normally do certain strokes easily and reliably does not necessarily mean that he could depend on his being able so to do them in exceptionally exciting circumstances. It is part of the interest of Croquet that one has to take into account one's own psychological make-up, and, of course, that of one's opponent also.

By the by, when laying a break be careful to make sure that your opponent's balls—that is, if you have touched them—have open shots. Again and again a player has come to grief by laying his break most beautifully, and then hearing the opponent say, sweetly: "I don't think I've got a shot," which usually means that he can lift his ball and get an easy roquet!

Here is something that reminds one that in Croquet constant vigilance, close observation, concentrated attention are essential for success.

XVIII

THE TAKING OF BISQUES

WHEN a player is in receipt of one bisque from an opponent who is only slightly better than himself, unless both are in the neighbourhood of being first-class, it will be both natural and correct to hold that bisque back until the end of the game, in the hope that at the critical moment it will just turn the scale.

Unfortunately, because in most cases one bisque should be held back for the end of the game, many players seem to have the idea that bisques should always be held back for some purely hypothetical psychological moment, which in point of fact never arrives.

A bisque, far from being a wonderful treasure to be carefully preserved and used only in the very last resort for purposes of defence, is a weapon that should be used with all reasonable speed for purposes of attack.

Suppose you are in receipt of a "pot of bisques" from a first-class player. Try and get the innings by all means in the ordinary way, but if you do not get it right away, take a bisque at once. Use one bisque to lay your break carefully, then follow it up with another to start your break. If you break down take a third.

If you have bisques left, and break down, always ask yourself this question: "Can I hope for a better opportunity of taking a bisque than the one I have now?" If you have stuck in a hoop, and there is a ball near you, another in the middle of the ground, and your pioneer-ball duly placed at the next hoop, there can be only one answer to this question. If you do not take your bisque when absolutely everything is thus set fair for you, you will certainly never have a better opportunity of taking one. And yet, how often have we known a long-bisquer—as players with many bisques are called—look a moment or two at such a situation, and then say, foolishly, "I don't think I will take another," and walk off the Court? This, of course, is the direct way to disaster.

In contrast, the sort of high bisquer who will quickly lose his or her bisques and become a better player will go ahead

TAKING OF BISQUES

and take the bisques, and try and win the game with their help as quickly as possible.

Here we must mention a very big error that is often made in the taking of bisques, even by those who ought to know better. If you fail in approaching a hoop, it seldom pays to use a bisque just to play your ball into position. It is usually better to go to some other ball. Take the following example. Red is two feet from the First Corner on the long boundary. Yellow is at the Third Hoop. Blue approaches the Second Hoop on Black and fails to get position. He then considers two possibilities. Shall he play behind Black, etc., and approach the Hoop again? Shall he just play into position? It is quite likely that that is what he will decide to do! He won't even look at Red. What he should do in such circumstances is to take a shot into the First Corner, actually at Red, if he has not roqueted it already. He can then take his bisque, and rush Red up the ground, and he has a Four Ball Break, and he has gained it with a minimum of risk, because even a raw beginner can bang a ball into a corner!

The moral is that when you have still a shot in hand, and are about to take a bisque, always let your imagination extend to any ball that is on, or quite close to a boundary. Do not waste a great opportunity of improving the whole lay-out by contenting yourself with just dribbling in front of your hoop, or to some ball just because it is near you.

By the by, when you are receiving odds from a better player it is up to you to make it quite clear when you intend to take a bisque, and to see that your opponent realizes that you are taking one. So long as you are on the Court your right to take a bisque remains, unless you have declared that you won't take one. As soon as you have walked off the Court your right to take a bisque has gone. But if you have declared that you *will* take a bisque, and wish to change your mind, you are at liberty to do so, and you cannot be compelled to take a bisque just because you have announced that you will. It is the duty of the giver-of-odds to record the bisques taken, and to let you know how many you have left, if you ask him; so, once more, be sure to make it known to your opponent when you are about to take a bisque, and on no account adopt that most reprehensible practice of just taking the bisque without a word or sign! This is the kind of thing that leads to absolutely unnecessary and futile trouble.

By the by, as at the moment we are advising the absolute beginner, and as when a foul has been committed it is often an appropriate moment to retrieve the situation with a bisque, we would just say: Do not get "hot and bothered" because your opponent suggests that you are about to play a stroke that might be a foul, and therefore it should be watched by a referee. This is the normal course of things. But you have the right to make sure that the person called to watch the stroke is a duly qualified referee, and not just anyone who happens to be available. And remember that a foul is not a Croquet crime, it is merely an ordinary failure to do something. Supposing, for example, that you are close to a hoop but much on the side. It is the sort of stroke that should be watched by a referee. Possibly you may make a perfectly correct stroke but stick in the hoop. You may, however, drive your ball through the hoop, but as your mallet-head was in contact with the ball when the ball hit the hoop upright the referee will adjudge it to be a foul. The one is no more a crime than the other. In both cases you have failed to run the hoop! Disappointing, perhaps, but nothing more. By the by, in this particular instance, unless absolutely driven to it by circumstances, you would probably be well advised not to take a bisque, as if you have made a crush you might waste your bisque by making another. But bear in mind that making a foul in no wise deprives you of the right to take a bisque, and in very many cases—such, for example, as having played with the wrong ball, or failed to shake the croqueted ball in Taking-off—you would be well advised at once to retrieve the situation by taking a bisque. We would again remind the beginner that a foul is not a croquet crime; and therefore if a foul is given against him he has no reason either to be ashamed or aggrieved; but he should note what happened in order, if possible, to avoid a like mistake another time.

XIX
DOUBLES

In many cases the only advice that it is necessary to give to the beginner or medium player about Doubles is obey your captain, on whose experience you must rely. If he does not know your play it is permissible, of course, for you to give him or her information about what you can do, or are afraid of. But, having given such information, you must try your best to carry out his or her instructions.

Often, however, Double Partners are much of a muchness, and though usually it is better that there should be a captain, some players play so well together, and are so accustomed to each other's play, that though there is an occasional "committee" on a difficult point, in the main each plays his or her own game.

In cases then when there is nearly equality between the partners, or at all events no great gap, and responsibility for direction is shared, we would respectfully urge that "committees" should be of as short duration as possible. We have most of us suffered at times from meeting opponents in doubles whose consultations were altogether unduly prolonged. In many cases it is quite obvious what must be done, and prolonged talk cannot alter the fact. In such cases to weary your opponents by over-long delays amounts, however unintentionally, to unfairness.

By the by, how very often we have heard people say: "Oh, if I had been playing a Single, I should have done so and so; but as it was a Double I had to think of my partner!" This idea, of course, is quite correct up to a point, but it can easily be carried too far. Surely what your partner will most appreciate is your playing well, and you are not at all likely to play well if you suddenly begin in a Double to play an altogether different type of game from what you would play in a Single.

One last word on Doubles, and it is this. You and your partner are a "team" both anxious to play well, both anxious to win; each doing his or her best; each disappointed if he or she makes a mistake; therefore if the game should be lost do not go round the ground attributing the blame to your partner.

It is more than likely that if you fairly considered matters you would find that you yourself were partly at fault; in any case your remedy is not to go round the ground condemning your partner, but to look out for a better partner for next time.

By the bye, the partner who breaks down, and whose break down causes the loss of the game, is not always by any means the culprit. Very often the trouble has been that his or her partner laid the break so badly that that was the real cause of the disaster. When, therefore, you are laying a break for your partner—unless you are an expert and your partner an absolute beginner—always be sure to go into committee so as to lay the break as your partner would like it. And if you know that your partner is nervous and over-anxious, be specially careful to give an easy " get away."

The art, of course, of nursing a weak partner consists mainly in again and again giving an easy " get away." It need hardly be emphasized that it is extremely important to give encouragement to the weak partner, and to discount undue dismay when the inevitable occasional break down does occur.

XX

PRACTICE

As in other arts more important than playing Croquet, much valuable time may be wasted by want of a good discretion in practice. For example, when once the Four Ball Break has been thoroughly mastered, it is waste of time to continue monotonously practising it. Instead concentrate on the Three Ball Break. If you can do a Three Ball Break well, you need have no fear about the Four Ball Break. Then do not forget to practise picking up breaks from difficult positions, changing a Three Ball Break into a Four Ball Break, and laying the break.

As you progress you will find that you master some strokes far more easily than others. Concentrate on the strokes in which you are weak.

It should be remembered that the Croquet player's most important asset in a tournament game is his confidence, and confidence is produced only by the knowledge that he is equal to the task before him; he will then say to himself, "I can do this!"

Now a player's knowledge that he is equal to the task before him, granted that he has mastered the principles of break making, etc., will mainly depend on the number of strokes that he can do with ease and assurance. Therefore practise with a view to increasing the number of strokes that you can do with ease and assurance.

Players are often heard lamenting that their play does not improve as they would like it to. Probably in many cases the reason is simply this, that they have not troubled to master the ordinary standard strokes of the game.

It is certain that there are many players who can do a Four Ball Break fairly well, who are yet very deficient outside that monotonous evolution.

An excellent way of spending a spare half-hour on the Croquet Lawn is to practise the Three Ball Break, making things as easy as possible, *but not taking advantage of the ease when made.* When you have run the first hoop, and have a nice

PRACTICE

comfortable Rush up the ground, don't take it! Instead do the long Split Roll. After the second hoop, do the long Split Drive to the third and fourth hoops! After the third hoop do the long Split Pass Roll. These are not easy strokes, and the last is a genuinely difficult one, but they are strokes that every ambitious player should try and master!

If you neglect to practise these and similar strokes you will suddenly find yourself faced with one in an important tournament game, and instead of being able to say to yourself, "I can do this!" you will have the cold comfort of the knowledge that you know nothing about it, and you will probably make a bungling attempt and come to hopeless grief.

Apart from any attempt to make a break, for the training of eye and hand, six to eight yard roquets; hoop-running from a yard to two or three yards; and hoop approaching from any and every position, should be specially and frequently practised.

In conclusion, we would once more urge: Concentrate on the strokes in which you are weak!

It is quite possible to be hours on the lawn playing strokes that you can do comfortably, without gaining much advantage; whereas a few minutes spent on those strokes about which you are doubtful would be far more useful.

Remember that to improve your game and chances of success you must increase and increase the number of strokes you can do with ease and certainty, and in so doing increase your confidence.

NOTE

We strongly urge all players to join the Croquet Association, and to compete in tournaments. By so doing you will not only be taking your share of responsibility for the general prosperity of the game, but you will add greatly to the pleasure of your practice, and gain an entrance into that body of pleasant and friendly people known as the "Croquet World"!

We would also urge players who are not already members of a Croquet Club to join one. Any doubt as to which Club may be most available can at once be set at rest by applying to the Secretary of the Croquet Association.